*The judicial response to the New Deal*

*This book is dedicated to my wife Susan
and to my children Alice, Adam and Eleanor*

*Richard A. Maidment*

# The judicial response
# to the New Deal

The US Supreme Court
and economic regulation, 1934–1936

MANCHESTER UNIVERSITY PRESS
Manchester and New York

Distributed exclusively in the USA and Canada by St. Martin's Press

Copyright © Richard A. Maidment 1991

*Published by* Manchester University Press
Oxford Road, Manchester M13 9PL, England
*and* Room 400, 175 Fifth Avenue, New York, NY 10010, USA

*Distributed exclusively in the USA and Canada*
*by* St. Martin's Press, Inc., 175 Fifth Avenue, New York, NY 10010, USA

*A catalogue record for this book is available from the British Library*

*Library of Congress cataloging in publication data*
Maidment, R. A. (Richard A.)
    The judicial response to the New Deal : the United States Supreme
Court and economic regulation, 1934–1936 / Richard A. Maidment.
        p.    cm.
    Includes bibliographical references and index.
    ISBN 0–7190–3332–2 (hardback)
    1. Industrial laws and legislation—United States—History—20th
century.    2. United States, Supreme Court—History—20th century.
3. Political questions and judicial power—United States–
–History—20th century.    4. Industry and state—United States–
–History—20th century.    5. New Deal, 1933–1939.    6. United States–
–Economic policy—1933–1945.    I. Title.
KF1600.M35    1991
343.73'07—dc20
[347.3037]                                                                                    91–17798

ISBN 0 7190 3332 2 *hardback*

Photoset in Linotron Janson
by Northern Phototypesetting Co, Ltd.
Printed in Great Britain
by Billings of Worcester

# Contents

# Preface

I have embarked on this book with an interesting blend of enthusiasm and reluctance. My enthusiasm is derived from the main premise of this book that the the response of the United States Supreme Court to the New Deal has been misunderstood. It has been misunderstood to the point that there are few if any scholars who do not accept the view that the Supreme Court, or at least the majority who controlled the Court, was driven by a combination of political prejudice and an absence of judicial integrity. I do not share this belief and I am delighted to have this opportunity to suggest that there are other explanations of the Court's decisions: explanations that are not located in the realm of judicial hostility and political spite. It has also been a unusual experience, both rewarding and slightly unnerving, to pursue this line of argument almost exclusively. Indeed, my sense of hesitation in embarking on this project is related to this experience. I am aware, after earlier articles on this subject, that this attempt to offer a different account of the Supreme Court's response to the New Deal will be viewed by some as an apology for the Court's majority. Perhaps it will seen by others as an indication of an absence of enthusiasm, on my part, for the early New Deal measures. I would like to make it clear that these have not been considerations, to the best of my knowledge, in the writing of this book. I do believe that the Court's record has been misunderstood, but that should not be taken to mean that I endorse the collective decisions of the majority, which in several instances were not as skilful or creative as they could have been. However, the absence of skill and creativity should not be equated with judicial partiality or the implementation of political preferences. Nor am I operating an undisclosed agenda, which seeks to dismiss the early New Deal as unsatisfactory or inadequate. I do not take a view in this book on the political and economic wisdom of the measures, although I do believe that the Roosevelt administration did not consider properly the full constitutional implications of its legislative programme and subsequently adopted a wholly unrealistic expectation of the programme's judicial prospects. It was an expectation that was always likely to be a source of frustration and anger for the administration, when it did not come to pass. However, I will now leave these prior explanations at this point and let the reader decide the strengths of the arguments deployed.

I do not wish to associate anyone else with the views that are displayed in this book, but I do need to thank several people without whom this book could not have been written. My greatest intellectual debt is to Professor William Letwin, formerly of the London School of Economics, who introduced me to the Supreme Court when I was an undergraduate at that institution. He was both an exceptional teacher and an outstanding scholar. He has also been, in the intervening years, exceptionally generous with his advice and time. This book owes him more than I can measure and more than words can express.

I would also like to thank Professor David Adams of the David Bruce Centre at the University of Keele, whose knowledge of the New Deal is encyclopaedic. I learnt a great deal from him about the early years of the first Roosevelt administration. I also owe a debt to Professor Maurice Vile, formerly of the University of Kent, for his patience in debating about the Supreme Court with someone far less experienced than he and with whom he clearly disagreed. Dr Alec Barbrook of the University of Kent has always been supportive and helpful, even when he did not share the same views. I would also like to thank the many students, undergraduate and graduate, who listened with patience to my views on the New Deal Court and then made me consider and refine them over the years.

I would also like to thank Dr Ian Bell, Dr Robert Garson and Dr Charles Swann, all of the University of Keele and all good friends, whose constant encouragement to complete an earlier draft of this book was, if not entirely welcome at the time, certainly appreciated after the event. Finally, my greatest debt is to my wife Susan. I will not expand on this here but she will know what I mean.

*Richard Maidment*

Milton Keynes, 1990

# 1

# Introduction

This book is primarily concerned with the response of the United States Supreme Court to the New Deal in the years until 1936. It seeks to provide another view of an episode that is seen by most students of the judicial process as settled. However, before the book proceeds to deal with these events, it is important to establish the wider reference and context within which I have approached this task. I bring to this study of the judicial response to the New Deal a particular understanding of the judicial process which differs to some extent from the view that is widely expressed. The literature on the judicial process, in both law and political science over the past few decades, has shown considerable certainty over explanations of judicial behaviour. It is no longer a difficult or almost impenetrable task to explain judicial behaviour. It is not, in Winston Churchill's words about Soviet foreign policy, 'a riddle wrapped in a mystery inside an enigma'. Rather, most scholars view judges as another variant of the species *homo politicus*. Judges are labelled conservative or liberal, or some point in between. Their decisions are analysed and located on a conventional political spectrum. The debates, in the scholarly literature, of course, are more sophisticated than those which occur in newspapers, but by and large they both share the view that judicial behaviour is understandable as a function of a judge's politics. In other words there is little that distinguishes the judicial function from the activity of politics, or judges from legislators. To some extent this book seeks to evaluate the nature of this perception, and the judicial response to the New Deal offers a particularly.fertile field for such an evaluation. The cases that have been chosen are from the early New Deal period culminating in *Carter* v. *Carter Coal Co.*, [1] the case that decided the fate of the Bituminous Coal Conservation Act of 1935.

1

These cases are all concerned with the constitutional validity of governmental intervention, both state and federal, in the nation's economic life. In each of these decisions the Supreme Court attempted to establish the perimeters of governmental authority in the field of economic regulation. It was, of course, a profoundly difficult task which the Court grappled with unsuccessfully from the end of the Civil War until the 1940s when it simply absolved itself from this burden. But one significant fact about these economic regulation cases, especially the early New Deal decisions, is that they are often proffered as evidence to substantiate the view of the judicial process that sees judges as politicians in judicial robes.

This book has two other concerns, but they are of such substantial dimensions that they can only be alluded to in this study. The first is that any theory of judicial motivation must be flexible enough to recognise the very real differences that exist between judges. Judges do pay homage to different gods, and not only political deities. For example, Mr Justice Stone and Mr Justice Sutherland, whose political views were broadly similar, nevertheless had very different conceptions of the legal process and the judicial function. How does one account for these differences? Why were there these contrasting beliefs held by the two men? The answer, partly, lies in the turmoil and tension within the legal profession in the 1930s. The broader answer lies in a study, for want of a better phrase, of the process through which lawyers and judges are socialised. Clearly this book is not the appropriate place for such a study but nevertheless it is a subject which cannot be entirely ignored within this context.

The second concern is of even greater importance. By what criteria should the judiciary exercise its very considerable powers within the American constitutional framework? Mr Justice Stone passionately wrote in *US* v. *Butler* that the 'only check upon our own exercise of power is our own sense of self-restraint'.[2] Stone clearly intended those words to be an admonition to the Court's 'conservatives' and in due course one of them, Mr Justice Sutherland, took the opportunity to reply in *West Coast Hotel* v. *Parrish*: 'The suggestion that the only check upon the exercise of the judicial power, when properly invoked, to declare a constitutional right superior to an unconstitutional statute is the judge's own faculty of self-restraint is both ill conceived and mischievous. Self-restraint belongs in the domain of will and not of judgement.'[3] In a sense Sutherland was quite right. Self-restraint *per se* does not provide the criterion for the exercise of the judicial power. Indeed, self-restraint for its own sake can produce an unsatisfactory result by unnecessarily inhibiting a judge. The critical problem, then, is developing criteria which will make it possible to judge when the judicial power is being abused. However, Sutherland, who correctly dismisses Stone's plea of self-restraint, does not provide an adequate alternative. 'The check upon the judge is that imposed by his oath of office, by the Constitution and by his own conscientious and enforced convictions.'[4] This unfortunately is not terribly useful. Conscientiousness, like self-restraint, does not belong in the realm of judgement. There is no societal benefit in a judge conscientiously implementing a foolish or improper standard which he personally cherishes. Thus the principal objective remains the development of standards for the exercise of the judicial power and then, but only then, the notion of conscientiousness can be introduced usefully.

So where does one start the search for these standards or criteria? Again this is a task which is far too substantial to be resolved here, nor is it the central concern of this book. However, it is a subject which cannot be entirely avoided.

## II

If there is one characteristic that distinguishes the activity of a judge from that of a politician it lies in the importance of legal rules and the extent to which pre-existing rules, or precedent, govern or restrict the process of judicial decision-making. Jurisprudentially the role of precedent in judicial decision-making has been a vexed question. Throughout the eighteenth and nineteenth centuries, a formalistic and mechanical explanation of law in general and the judicial role in particular prevailed in the Anglo-American legal world. The law was viewed as a 'body of general rules (a major premise) from which, by a process of deduction (after the introduction of a minor premise) any specific controversy would be correctly solved through arriving at a more specific rule which would determine the proper immediate solution'.[5] Within this framework the task of a judge, through his legal skills, was to discover the appropriate rules which governed the facts at hand. According to this mode of thought the decision of a court was merely the mechanical result of the application of antecedent rules to the facts of the particular case. The most celebrated exponent of this version of the judicial process in Anglo-American jurisprudence was Sir William Blackstone. In his *Commentaries on the Laws of England*, he wrote:

> The judgement though pronounced or awarded by the judges is not their determination or sentence, but the determination and sentence of law. It is the conclusion that naturally and regularly follows from the premises of law and fact . . . which judgement or conclusion depends not therefore on the arbitrary caprice of the judge, but the settled and invariable principles of justice.[6]

Blackstone's enormous influence can be assessed by the fact that virtually two centuries later, Mr Justice Roberts, speaking for the United States Supreme Court, appeared to reiterate these beliefs in a version only slightly modified to take account of the specifics of the American legal process. Roberts wrote in *US* v. *Butler*: 'When an act of Congress is appropriately challenged in the courts as not conforming to the constitutional mandate the judicial branch has only one duty – to lay the article of the Constitution which is invoked beside the statute which is challenged and to decide whether the latter squares with the former.'[7] This appearance of serene continuity in the belief that judges were merely the passive instrument through which the correct legal rule would be enunciated belied the existence of a bitter controversy in the American legal profession over the previous forty years. Indeed it was ironic that Roberts' remarks were made in the decade when the American legal realist movement came to fruition.

The genesis of the realist movement's attitude to precedent can be discerned in the writings and practices of Oliver Wendell Holmes and Benjamin Cardozo. Both of them were profoundly sceptical of a mechanistic jurisprudence and they used their considerable authority as appellate and ultimately United States Supreme Court justices to suggest that judges were susceptible to subjective influences. This is a theme which was constantly present in Holmes' writings and opinions. Holmes continually used to remind his brethren on the Supreme Court that their judgements could well be influenced by factors outside the legal realm and that their decisions could be the product of the 'conscious result of subjective pressures and inarticulate convictions'.[8] He furthermore was sceptical of the efficacy of rules in guiding a judge in any particular case. As he wrote in *Lochner* v. *New York*, '[g]eneral propositions do not determine concrete cases'.[9] He elaborated on this sentiment to Harold Laski: 'I always say in conference that no case can be settled by general propositions, that I will admit any general proposition you like and decide the case either way.'[10] In these remarks, Holmes appeared to be suggesting that when judges desire a conclusion from a proposition, they have in fact also introduced a mediating assumption which may or may not be visible. Furthermore it is usually this assumption, not necessarily of a legal nature, which has guided the overt logic in the opinion to the desired conclusion. Holmes was not reticent in unmasking these assumptions which he believed underpinned the formal logic of his colleagues' opinions. He did so, for example, in *Lochner* with the now classic statement: 'The Fourteenth Amendment did not enact Mr Herbert Spencer's Social Statics.'[11] Holmes clearly believed that Mr Justice Peckam's majority opinion was disingenuously simple in an area where legal and constitutional authority were at best obscure. As a result Peckham's opinion, to Holmes, was indulging in a subterfuge in order to disguise its true motivation – the protection of vested interests. Throughout his career Holmes maintained this attack against a mechanistic jurisprudence. His opinions are tangibly different from most of his judicial brethren especially in his early years on the Supreme Court. Where theirs were marked by certainty and rectitude, his opinions were charac-terised by scepticism and a measure of uncertainty. The achievement of the man is that, by the end of his career, he had demonstrated convincingly the inadequacies of a 'slot-machine' jurisprudence and had established that judges were affected by 'unconscious preferences', 'inarticulate convictions', and a host of other non-legal factors. In 1941 Moses Aronson claimed that 'his [Holmes'] influence upon contemporary legal thought is reminiscent of the effect which Kant had upon the development of philosophy in the nineteenth century'.[12] Perhaps Aronson was guilty of hyperbole, but his remark does illustrate the regard in which he was, and indeed still is, held by an extraordinarily wide spectrum of legal opinion. Many of the recurrent themes present in Holmes' opinions are also present in the writings of Benjamin Cardozo. The most comprehensive and cogent statement of Cardozo's conception of the judicial process is to be found in the Storrs lectures delivered at Yale University in 1921.[13] At the time he was a member of the Supreme Court of the State of New York and was thus able to illustrate his ideas from his experiences as an appeal court judge. Cardozo commenced his lectures with an attempt to delineate the subjective influences that Holmes had talked about:

> ... there is in each of us a stream of tendency ... which gives coherence and direction to thought and action. Judges cannot escape that current any more than other mortals. All their lives forces which they do recognise and cannot name have been tugging at them ... and the resultant is an outlook on life, a conception of social needs ... which, when reasons are nicely balanced must determine where choice must fall.[14]

As Cardozo perceived the problem there was a twofold aspect to a judge's work in cases where the legal authority is equivocal. Firstly, he must establish the *ratio decidendi*, the underlying principle of the most pertinent precedental case. Secondly, the judge must extend this principle along a particular path in order to provide the most amenable solution to the issue under consideration. The path chosen, according to Cardozo, is not solely affected, nor should it be, by legal criteria. In his words:

> The directive force of a principle may be extended along the line of a logical progression, this I will call the rule of analogy or the method of philosophy; along the line of historical development ... the method of evolution; along the line of customs of the community ... the method of tradition; along the lines of justice, morals and social welfare, the mores of the day ... the method of sociology.[15]

However, having asserted his belief that judges were affected by subconscious factors and that furthermore they utilised modes of reasoning that were not legal, Cardozo went to great lengths to place these notions in perspective. He wrote:

> . . . a sketch of the judicial process which concerns itself almost exclusively with the creative and dynamic element, is likely to give an overcolored picture of uncertainty in the law and of free discretion in the judge. Of the cases that come before the Court in which I sit a majority I think could not with semblance of reason be decided in any way but one. The law and its appreciation alike are plain. Such cases are predestined, so to speak, to affirmance without opinion.[16]

Cardozo restated these sentiments even more emphatically: '. . . nine-tenths perhaps more of the cases that come before a court are predestined in a sense, that they are predestined – their fate pre-established by inevitable laws that follow them from birth to death.'[17] Because the Storrs lectures were principally concerned with an examination of extra-legal factors in judicial decisions, Cardozo's essentially cautious juristic beliefs are often over-looked. But the above remarks make it pellucid that he believed in the utility and efficiency of legal rules and that the judiciary should and indeed do treat them with respect. Cardozo thus was not attempting to dismiss the importance of legal rules, but was interested in exposing the rigidities and over-simplifications of Blackstonian jurisprudence. The model with which he wished to replace it was characterised by balance and tension. In the minority of cases that Cardozo spoke of where legal authority was equivocal, a judge's decision emerged from the balance and tension of legal and institutional factors on the one hand, and policy objectives on the other. The point where the balance was struck or the extent to which either element predominated varied from case to case and between judges. This model, Cardozo believed, was more congruent with reality than earlier versions of judicial decision-making. But it was precisely this subtle and delicate balance, posited by Cardozo, that American legal realism, or that part of the school dominated by Karl Llewellyn, sought to negate. The work of the American realists reflects the intellectual obligations owed to Holmes and Cardozo. They incorporate the insights of these two men in their writings. However, there are substantial differences between them and Cardozo and Holmes.

Their central dispute concerns the question of precedent. The most vigorous and fundamental critique of legal rules was developed by Karl Llewellyn.[18] Llewellyn's theory centred around a concept that is now referred to as 'rule-scepticism'. It is an extension of the doubts enunciated by Holmes and Cardozo about the efficiency of rules. However, it is so radical an extension that it is all but a concept of a different nature. Briefly stated, the precepts of rule-scepticism are firstly that there are a multiplicity of rules governing a single issue of law which is being contested. Cardozo made the very same point but limited the assertion to a small category of cases. By contrast, Llewellyn argued that this was true of all legal disputes which reached the stage of litigation. Secondly, there were a multiplicity of techniques to interpret precedent. In his book, *The Common Law Tradition*, Llewellyn listed 'sixty-four available precedent techniques',[19] techniques which Llewellyn argued provided judges with a legitimate vehicle for evading the apparent implication of previous rules. Thirdly, there is the question of legal language, which realists argue obfuscates the issues and make it possible to increase even further the number of interpretations, including contradicting ones, available to a judge. Jerome Frank claimed: 'in the last ten years or so Leon Green, Walter Cook and Thurman Arnold and others of us . . . undertook the dissection of legal terminology. We skinned the peel off much legal jargon, many words (not all of course); they proved to be like onions, you peeled and there was nothing left.'[20] The inevitable conclusion that Llewellyn and the other realists arrived at was that in any legal conflict which reaches the stage of litigation, there would be *at least two* different and legally correct solutions available to a judge. A judge could only decide between the array of possible responses by using extra-legal criteria. The type of extra-legal factors Llewellyn had in mind emerged in his writings on prediction and judicial decisions. He suggested that if a pattern could be detected in a particular judge's career, then the regularity was due to 'the reaction of judges to the fact and to the life around them'.[21] Fred Rodell, another leading realist, articulated these sentiments more forcefully: 'The vote of each Supreme Court justice however rationalised à la mode, however fitted afterward into the pigeon hole of some politico-juridical principle, has rather been the result of a vast complex of personal factors – temperament, background, education, economic status, pre-court career . . .'.[22] Other realists might well add to or subtract from Rodell's list, but all the rule-sceptic school would accept the authenticity of his underlying assumptions. They would approve his emphasis on personal factors and the consequent dismissal of legal and institutional influences. It was this understanding of legal rules that judicial behaviouralists adopted.

Interestingly the other major strand of realism, fact-scepticism, which coexists uneasily with rule-scepticism, has not been adopted by the behaviouralist movement. Indeed it has almost entirely been ignored. Yet it shares the same basic motivating and driving force of rule-scepticism although it comes to very different conclusions. Fact-scepticism, which is virtually the personal creation of Jerome Frank, developed from his instinct that the rule-sceptics had distorted the picture of the legal process by concentrating exclusively on appellate courts.[23] If, Frank argued, they had examined the workings of trial courts their conclusions would have been substantially different. In Frank's view the problem of deciding the governing legal rule in a case was not a problem at all to a trial court judge. The operative rule was rarely questioned. Rather it was the facts that were always at the centre of a controversy. The essence of fact-scepticism is captured in the following passage:

> Most law suits, are in part at least, 'fact suits'. The facts are past events . . . The trial judge or jury endeavouring . . . to learn those past events, must rely, usually, on the oral testimony of witnesses who say they observed these events. The several witnesses usually tell conflicting stories. This must mean that at least some of the witnesses are either (a) lying or (b) were honestly mistaken in recollecting their observations or (c) are honestly mistaken in narrating their recollections at the trial . . . The trial court judge or jury must select some part of the conflicting testimony to be treated as reliably reporting the past facts. In each law suit, that choice of what is deemed reliable testimony depends upon the unique reactions of a particular trial judge or a particular jury to the particular witnesses who testify in that particular suit. The choice is consequently discretionary: the trial court exercises 'fact-discretion'.[24]

From this analysis Frank came to certain conclusions. The first, which is of considerable importance but not entirely germane to the discussion at hand, is that trial courts were unable to recreate the original situation and thus unable to mete out justice. Secondly, and more relevantly, Frank discounted the claim that a pattern could be observed in the behaviour of judges as the fact situation was too random to permit such a pattern to develop: 'Since most persons consider that a true science makes prediction possible, we ought to put an end to notions of 'legal science' . . . because no formula for predicting most trial court decisions can be devised which does not contain hopelessly numerous variables that cannot be pinned or correlated.'[25]

Perhaps given these beliefs it is not surprising that most judicial behaviouralists have ignored the corpus of Frank's work. They cannot however ignore it quite that easily. For Frank initially was not a fact-sceptic. There is no real reference to it in the 1930s.[26] Frank's fact-scepticism developed after his experience as a trial court judge. Interestingly, none of the other realists who disputed the validity of fact-scepticism even sat on the bench. Furthermore, Frank had originally accepted the tenets of rule-scepticism but qualified his acceptance by denying its applicability to trial courts. Possibly as a result of his judicial experience he came to believe that rule-scepticism did not accurately portray the work of appellate courts either. He came to believe that rules did play an important, indeed at times a completely determinative role in appellate courts. The reason he gave for this change was that facts determine the legal rule, that judges apply and that the evaluation of facts is carried out by trial courts. Therefore appellate courts have no difficulty in determining the appropriate rule for the facts have been 'authoritatively established' by the trial court.

Despite Frank's credentials as a realist his criticism of rule-scepticism has not been seriously weighed by the discipline of political science. Rather, it has been glossed over. Frank, like other critics of rule-scepticism, has essentially been ignored and his opinions have not been taken into account. Rather, the 'truth' of rule-scepticism has been accepted by most political scientists in its entirety. The delicate balance postulated by Cardozo and Holmes has been ignored by the political science profession. Rule-scepticism was adopted almost by stealth, which is unfortunate for only when legal rules are dismissed as having no part to play in judicial decision-making should the search commence for other factors which will explain judicial behaviour. Political scientists have concentrated on developing increasingly sophisticated methodologies to study judicial behaviour, while not engaging in debate over the fundamental and critical assumptions of rule-scepticism. Thus the subsequent chapters will address themselves to the validity of this critical premise in the context of the Supreme Court's response to the early New Deal.

**NOTES**

1 298 US 238 (1936).
2 297 US 1, 78 (1936).
3 300 US 379, 402 (1937).
4 *Ibid.*, p. 402.
5 T. L. Becker, *Political Behaviouralism and Modern Jurisprudence*, (1964), p. 42.
6 W. Blackstone, *Commentaries on the Laws of England*, Volume 3 (1821), p. 434.
7 297 US 1, 62 (1936).
8 O. W. Holmes, *The Common Law* (1881), p. 36.
9 198 US 45, 76 (1905).
10 M. D. Howe (ed.), *Holmes-Laski Letters: The Correspondence of Mr. Justice Holmes and Harold J. Laski*, Volume 1 (1953), p. 243.
11 198 US 45, 75 (1905).
12 M. Aronson, 'Tendencies in American jurisprudence', 4 *University of Toronto Law Journal* 92, 93 (1941). Holmes' historical reputation rests on his career as a judge, rather than on his writings as a legal philosopher where he attempted to develop his own version of legal positivism. Apart from his *The Common Law*, p. 36, note 8, see 'The path of the law', 10 *Harvard Law Review* 458 (1987). For a discussion of Holmes' positivism see M. Howe, 'The positivism of Mr Justice Holmes', 64 *Harvard Law Review* 530 (1951); H. Hart, 'Holmes's positivism – an addendum', *Ibid.*, p. 930; and M. Howe, 'Holmes's positivism – a brief rejoinder', *Ibid.*, p. 938.
13 These lectures were published in *The Nature of the Judicial Process* (1921).
14 *Ibid.*, p. 12.
15 *Ibid.*, pp. 30, 31.
16 *Ibid.*, p. 149
17 M. Hall (ed.), *Selected Writings of Benjamin Nathan Cardozo* (1947), p. 13.
18 See Llewellyn's principal works, K. Llewellyn, *The Bramble Bush: On Our Law and its Study* (1960); *The Common Law Tradition* (1960); *Jurisprudence: Realism in Theory and Practice* (1962). For a sympathetic evaluation of Llewellyn, see W. Twining, *Karl Llewellyn and the Realist Movement* (1973).
19 Llewellyn, *The Common Law Tradition*, p. 76.
20 J. Frank, 'A lawyer looks at language', in S. L. Hayakawa (ed.), *Language in Action* (1941), p. 329.
21 Llewellyn, *Jurisprudence*, p. 76.

22 F. Rodell, 'For every justice judicial deference is a sometime thing', 50 *Georgetown Law Journal* 700, 701 (1962).

23 Frank's major works are J. Frank, *Law and the Modern Mind* (1930 and 1963); *Courts on Trial: Myth and Reality in American Justice* (1949). For a concise but intelligent evaluation of Frank, see E. Cahn, *Confronting Injustice* (1967), pp. 265–315.

24 Quoted in Cahn, *Confronting Injustice*, p. 285.

25 Quoted in W. Rumble Jr., *American Legal Realism*, p. 126.

26 The change in Frank's approach is apparent from the differences between the two editions of his book, *Law and the Modern Mind*, *op. cit.*, note 23.

# 2

# The Supreme Court and economic regulation

The iconography of the United States Supreme Court in the first part of the 1930s is well established. The heroes, the villains and the not so villainous are familiar. On the one hand there are Justices Brandeis, Cardozo and Stone, and on the other there are the 'four horsemen of reaction', Justices Butler, McReynolds, Sutherland and Van Devanter. Occupying the middle ground, a position which does not have any of the normal connotations of political virtue and good sense, are Justices Roberts and Hughes. The 'liberal three', the 'conservative four' and the swingmen is the most common and indeed the standard interpretation of the Court's behaviour in the 1930s, *vide* Arthur Schlesinger Jr.:

> Nonetheless Van and Mac – Willis Van Devanter and James C. McReynolds – were still there along with Butler and Sutherland, a compact group of four always able to outvote the three liberals – old man Holmes (replaced in 1932 in Benjamin N. Cardozo), Brandeis and Stone. In the centre holding the balance of power, stood Hughes and Roberts.[1]

But just in case the reader may feel that this is a too dispassionate or neutral analysis of the Court, Schlesinger quotes Thomas Reed Powell to demonstrate which side he is on:

> The four stalwarts differ among themselves in temperament. I think that Mr. Justice Butler knows just what he is up to and that he is playing God or Lucifer to keep the world from going the way he does not want it to. Sutherland seems to me a naive, doctrinaire person who really does not know the world as it is. His incompetence in economic reasoning is amazing. . . . Mr. Justice McReynolds is a contemptuous cad and Mr. Justice Van Devanter is an old dodo.[2]

13

Powell's comments made in the 1930s on the 'conservatives' are harsh and particularly in the case of Van Devanter outrageously wrong, but they are not very different in kind or manner from other critiques of the Court. Pearson and Allen in another contemporaneous account refer to 'reactionary justices bent on legislative murder [who] count for more than three liberals, regardless how righteous their cause and how irrefutable their logic'.[3] In 1941, Robert H. Jackson, Attorney-General of the United States, wrote:

> [b]ut in striking at New Deal laws, the Court allowed its language to run riot. It attempted to engraft its own nineteenth-century *laissez-faire* philosophy upon a Constitution intended by its founders to endure for ages.... The Court not merely challenged the policies of the New Deal but enacted judicial barriers to the reasonable exercise of legislative powers, both state and national, to meet the urgent needs of a twentieth-century community.[4]

Justice Stone, writing to his sister in 1936, voiced similar sentiments:

> We finished the term of Court yesterday. I think in many ways one of the most disastrous in its history. At any rate it seems to me that the Court has been needlessly narrow and obscurantist in its outlook. ... Our latest exploit was a holding by a divided vote that there was no power in a state to regulate minimum wages for women. Since the Court last week[5] said that this could not be done by the national government as the matter was local, and now it said that it cannot be done by local governments even though it is local, we seem to have tied Uncle Sam up in a hard knot.'[6]

Nor has time softened the attitudes of commentators toward the 'conservatives'. Robert G. McCloskey, ironically in an essay urging the Warren Court to involve itself in the issues of economic due process refers to:

> a conservative majority [which] had, from time to time, embraced a policy of adamant resistance to economic experiment, and this obscurantist spirit had reached its zenith in the judicial reaction to the New Deal. ... That majority had raised a barrier, not only against particular features of the law, but 'against all legislative action of this nature by declaring that the subject matter itself lies beyond the reach' of governmental authority. This intransigence had tended to discredit the whole concept of judicial supervision in

the minds of those who felt government must have reasonable leeway to experiment with the economic order.[7]

Even Mr Justice Sutherland's biographer, J. F. Paschal, who is sympathetic to his subject talks of 'the failure . . . is not merely Sutherland's failure. If that were all we could forget him. It is the failure of American conservative thought since the Civil War. One of Sutherland's claims on our attention, therefore is as a representative of the conservative tradition.'[8]

Of course both legal realists and judicial behaviouralists have accepted and propagated this interpretation of the Court's actions. Fred Rodell, a leading realist writes about the nine justices in the following manner which makes no attempt to conceal his prejudices:

> Reading roughly and a bit perversely from right to left, . . . a first billing nationally goes to Van Devanter, McReynolds, Sutherland and Butler . . . whom New Dealers were soon to dub the Four Horsemen of Reaction, and who followed the narrow-gauge, anti-governmental *constitutional* slant of Thomas Jefferson, whose *political* purposes they would have loathed, instead of the broad-interpretation slant of Alexander Hamilton, whose politics they would have embraced. These were the men . . . who held the power to say No to the President, the Congress and the overwhelming majority of the nation. To do so, they needed only one more judicial recruit to the cause of reaction-in-the-name-of-the-Constitution – and they found him, until he turned coat on them two long years after he joined them, in Owen Roberts of Pennsylvania . . Hughes could scarcely look to any of the colleagues on his ideological right; the quixotically turn-back-the-clock quartet would give no inch in their creeds or convictions, come depression, panic or possible constitutional revolution; vacillating Roberts might be persuaded or pressured if things got uncomfortably hot, but he lacked the fortitude to help lead. For assistance, Hughes would have to look to his left, to . . . Brandeis, Stone and Cardozo.[9]

Rodell makes it lucidly clear that he is on the side of the angels, the 'liberal' angels, but interestingly although he disapproves of the 'conservatives' he is most contemptuous of the 'vacillating' Roberts. He virtually accuses Roberts of the 'switch in time that saved none'. C. Herman Pritchett also refers to 'Roberts' strange waverings and wanderings . . . the odd man of the Court, and to both Roberts and Hughes as 'falling somewhere between these two groups in their thinking and no one could predict how they would line up on particular legislative issues'.[10] Glendon Schubert using the Shapley-Shubik empirical power index to analyse 'the switch' during the 1936 Term describes it in the orthodox manner. 'During the 1936 Term, the Court was divided between a three-justice liberal bloc and a four-justice conservative bloc with Hughberts in the middle.'[11] After utilising the power index, Schubert concludes:

> The questions that we raised initially however, remain: Who switched? And why? . . . [There is] one interpretation of the events, and one possible answer to the questions: that *both* Hughes and Roberts switched in order to protect the institutional integrity and authority of the Supreme Court from the threatened much greater danger presented by the President's proposal to subject the Court to *external* political domination.'[12]

The issue of the switch in the aftermath of the court-packing furore is not a central concern of this book, indeed it has been dealt with conclusively elsewhere.[13] However it is hoped that the remarks quoted above, to which many others could easily have been added, will help to establish two things. First, there is a consensus about the Supreme Court in the early to middle 1930s. The above comments are drawn from very varied sources: journalists, a Supreme Court justice, the Attorney-General of the United States, a historian, lawyers, a traditional political scientist, a legal historian, judicial behaviouralists and a legal realist. They all share the belief that the 'conservative grouping' on the Court were politically motivated and that the explanation for their decisions must be sought in the justices' personal ideologies. Furthermore Hughes' and Roberts' behaviour, particularly the latter, can only be understood through a combination of ideological predilection and tactical voting. Secondly, the inferences drawn from this consensual belief diverge sharply. The realists and the behaviouralists expect judges to be motivated by a personal ideology and consequently the behaviour of the conservatives confirm their hypothesis. Indeed in their view, Brandeis, Cardozo and Stone behaved no differently. 'No less', writes Rodell, 'than McReynolds on the far side of the fence, did

Brandeis seek to write his own economic ideas into law.'[14] At this point the realists and the behaviouralists part company with the rest, who believe in a legal process with integrity, and consider that Butler *et al.*, with the assistance of Hughes and Roberts, violated this process. They read their preference for an individualistic and atavistic capitalism into the Constitution. By contrast, it is argued, Brandeis, Cardozo and Stone were not guilty of comparable behaviour; they did not implement their own societal views. A.T. Mason, the official biographer of Stone declares:

> Stone found little satisfaction in the New Deal. . . . Sharing the prejudices against Rooseveltian concoctions common to many good Republicans the Justice joined in ridiculing the 'professors' and the 'Brain Trust'. . . . 'I am wondering how you feel about this present day and age,' he asked an old-fashioned Democrat. 'Much of it seems incredible to me and especially our departure from traditional *methods* of dealing with public questions.' Fundamentally, he thought New Dealers prone to invoke the coercive sanctions of the community before allowing the intelligence and public spirit of responsible individuals opportunity to provide an enduring corrective.[15]

Instead of imposing their own views these three judges attempted to sustain their position through legal, constitutional and historical argument which did not offend the canons of judicial propriety. The most important point to recognise is that there is an understanding of judicial propriety at work here which by definition excludes the influence of personally-held beliefs on society and politics affecting the judicial decision-making process. So Butler *et al.* are not only being accused here of subscribing to a conservative ideology, which is the core of the realist complaint, but mainly of not being able to distinguish their politics from their judicial duty.

It is ironic that the first intimations of judicial reactions to the New Deal were 'hopeful'. They were 'hopeful' to the extent that some commentators detected a realignment on the Supreme Court, with Hughes and Roberts joining the 'liberal' bloc, thereby creating a five to four 'liberal' majority. The 'hopeful' signs, as we now know with hindsight, proved to be illusory, but the signs were never really very substantial and indeed, in retrospect, it does look like a case of wish fulfillment gone awry. The immediate cause for optimism was the Supreme Court's decisions in 1933–4 to sustain certain statutes which authorised state governments to intervene in the economy.[16] In *Minnesota* v. *Blasius*,[17] which dealt with the vexed question of state taxation and interstate commerce, the Supreme Court sustained the constitutionality of a state levy on cattle held inside the state for delivery within its borders after having been transported through interstate commerce.[18] In two far more important cases, *Home Building and Loan Association* v. *Blaisdell*[19] and *Nebbia* v. *New York*,[20] which will be discussed at length below, observers claimed that they could detect a relaxation of the constitutional limitations against governmental intervention in the economy. But, in fact, these cases were not amenable to such an interpretation. And the fact that they were not interpretable in such a manner should have been very clear from the previous sixty years.

Since the end of the Civil War, and more specifically since the passing of the Fourteenth Amendment, the courts had grappled with the issue of governmental regulation of the economy.[21] Indeed it would be no exaggeration to say that this was the central and dominating issue before the judiciary during the period. It was hardly surprising that this was the case, as the rapid industrialisation of the American economy had brought in its train a variety of social and economic problems. The federal and state governments, responding to pressures from their publics, passed, legislation which attempted to ameliorate the more deleterious effects of the new industrial order. For instance, bills establishing minimum wages and maximum hours were passed as were statutes regulating the prices that could be charged for a variety of goods and services.[22] The federal government imposed a tax on incomes above \$400 and attempted to eliminate child labour in factories.[23] The response from manufacturers, railroad companies and in general those who deemed themselves affected was to appeal to the courts and challenge the constitutionality of such legislation. These appeals were usually based on the due process of law clauses of the Fifth and Fourteenth Amendments, although other sections of the Constitution, the contract clause, the privileges and immunity clause of the Fourteenth Amendment, the taxing power and the Tenth amendment were often cited as the source of the constitutional challenge. Unfortunately for the courts the problem raised by these challenges was intractable; it did not lend itself to a universally or indeed widely accepted judicial solution. The issue was not amenable to the development of a judicial formula which could be readily applied to a wide variety of situations. If just the area of due process is briefly examined, the difficulties faced by the judiciary will be apparent.

The historiography of the period from the Civil War to the 1930s has a shared orthodoxy. Arthur Selwyn Miller, in his book *The Supreme Court and American Capitalism*, expresses this view cogently:

> The history of three-quarters of a century between the Civil War and 1937 may be seen as a contest between rugged individualism and a rising tide of equalitarianism. . . . During that time to put the matter as briefly as possible the High Bench, under the leadership of Stephen J. Field and such luminances of the American bar as Roscoe Conkling, constructed principles of laissez-faire and read them into the Constitution to protect both individual and corporate activity from governmental regulation.'[24]

Similarly Sidney Fine declares:

> It was in the courts that the idea of laissez-faire won its greatest victory in the three and one-half decades after the Civil War. Here, the laissez-faire views of academic and popular theorists and of practical businessmen were translated from theory into practice. Bar and bench joined forces in making laissez-faire an important element of constitutional doctrine and in establishing the courts as the ultimate censors of virtually all forms of social and economic legislation.'[25]

But Miller and Fine in fact oversimplify both the judicial and economic history of the period. As William Letwin points out:

> Economic doctrines have never as much influenced the making of American economic policy as have political and constitutional considerations. The reason why the whole of American economic policy looks so incoherent – with mercantilist, socialist liberal or autarkic elements all living happily side by side – is that political balance rather than economic consistency has been the more powerful drive.'[26]

And Letwin's point about incoherence and inconsistency can easily be transposed to judicial decision-making in the area of due process and economic regulation. The source of the judiciary's inconsistency, paradoxically, is due to the fact that judges were in broad agreement over the perimeters of judicial responsibility. Firstly, they accepted that government, state or federal, could not dispose of property, private or corporate, in any manner it thought appropriate. The mandates of the due process clause of both the Fifth and Fourteenth Amendment were understood by the courts to impose limitations on governmental intervention in private economic arrangements.[27] Secondly, virtually every judge who sat on the United States Supreme Court from the end of the Civil War accepted that government had certain police powers, which Chief Justice Taney described as 'nothing more or less than powers of government inherent in every sovereignty'.[28] Thus it was universally agreed that government, under the police power, had the constitutional authority to make regulations for the benefit of the health, welfare and moral well-being of its citizens. In order to achieve these objectives government had the power to curtail the freedom of contract and the disposal of private property. As Justice Sutherland noted: 'There is, of course, no such thing as absolute freedom of contract. It is subject to a great variety of restraints.'[29] Therein lay the crux of the judicial dilemma; private property is constitutionally safeguarded, but the protection is not absolute. Mr Justice Peckham, author of the infamous majority opinion in *Lochner* v. *New York*, [30] phrased it slightly differently: 'It is a question of which two powers or rights shall prevail, the power of the state to legislate or that of the individual to liberty of person or freedom of contract.'[31] Mr Justice Holmes would not have dissented from that analysis of the options facing the Court.

If it then was widely accepted that private property was constitutionally protected but not absolutely, the judiciary could not and indeed did not merely side with propertied interests against governmental regulations. Instead the courts attempted to develop a formula, a *modus vivendi* to achieve a balance between these values. The rate regulation cases, or the maximum hours for working men and women, will illustrate the judiciary's attempt to provide a solution. If the rate regulation issue is taken first, it is interesting to see how the Court approached the problem. Firstly, corporations, which owned railroads or grain elevators, were deemed to be entitled to constitutional protection. But secondly, after *Munn* v. *Illinois*,[32] industries such as the railroad industry were susceptible to governmental regulation. Thirdly, the regulation, however, had to be reasonable; it had to be a reasonable exercise of the police power. Inevitably the question of reasonableness became very vexed. Some judges, like Holmes, felt that perhaps the third stage of the reasoning process could be avoided by letting the legislature decide the question of reasonableness.[33] But others were reluctant to give this task to legislatures because they felt politicians might well abuse this power by effectively confiscating property. To elaborate further, the usual mode of governmental control was to establish a maximum price at which the industry could sell its services. Therefore the state-regulated price or rate would determine the percentage return on the industry's invested capital. So if the government's price levels were set too low the return on capital might be negligible or even non-existent. This would be tantamount, if not to confiscation, then to using private property without payment for that usage. If the courts decided not to examine the consequences of the governmentally-chosen price levels, then the judiciary could have been accused, and fairly, of taking away those constitutional protections with one hand which it had just endowed with the other. Chief Justice Waite, in a case sustaining the validity of a state regulation, felt obliged to point out:

> From what has been said it is not to be inferred that this power of limitation or regulation is itself without limit. This power to regulate is now a power to destroy, and limitation is not the equivalent of confiscation. Under pretence of regulating fares and freight the state cannot require a railroad corporation to carry persons or property without reward; neither can it do that which in law amounts to taking a private property for public use without just compensation, or without due process of law.[34]

Therefore the courts were compelled for reasons of logic to concern themselves with establishing the proper level of charges, only to discover immediately that it was an inordinate task. Mr Justice Harlan, considered a 'liberal', wrote the opinion which struck down a Nebraska statute because the rates set by the state did not permit an adequate return on investment. But if the Nebraska rate schedule did not permit a fair return on a fair valuation of the investment, the Court would have to decide the level of charges which would provide a fair return plus a method of calculating the capital invested. At this point, the Supreme Court, due to its lack of expertise, showed signs of distress. Harlan, referring to the problem of a fair valuation claimed that the following factors should be taken into account:

> The original cost of construction, the amount expended in permanent improvements, the amount and market value of its bonds and stocks, the present as compared with the original cost of construction, the probable earning capacity of the property under particular rates prescribed by statute, and the sum required to meet operating expenses, are all matters for consideration . . . we do not say that these may not be regarded in estimating the value of property.[35]

Furthermore, the question of what was a fair percentage return on the capital was still to be resolved. The *Minnesota Rate Case*[36] of 1890 posed the same problems, and as Arthur Sutherland has said:

> the *Minnesota Rate Case* . . . left the Court with a number of problems, all centring around the fact that, in plain terms, the decision sets the Supreme Court to re-deciding questions concerning the reasonableness of government measures . . . for example how will a court fix a standard for determining the fair value of a public utility system? No satisfactory answer has emerged in the . . . years since the *Minnesota Rate Case*.[37]

The courts indeed did not evolve an adequate answer to the problem, but as they had accepted the issue of rate regulation as justifiable the courts had to provide a judicial response. The response that emerged was not the coherent and consistent *laissez-faire* attitude ascribed by Fine and Miller, for more often than not governmental regulations were sustained. The response was inconsistent, varying from case to case-reflecting the judiciary's confusion plus the sheer difficulty of providing a satisfactory judicial solution to this issue.

The contentious issue of maximum hours for working men and women, also elicited a similarly ambivalent response from the courts. Again the courts felt that government could intervene in contractual arrangements between employer and employee, but not indiscriminately. The police power could be used to regulate the maximum number of hours worked to protect the health and welfare of the work-force in industry. But the judiciary at first would not allow governments to regulate the hours worked in all occupations. Instead judges insisted that industries should be treated singly and separately and that a specific health hazard, over and above the expected or average hazard to health from employment, had to be proven before they were prepared constitutionally to validate a governmental restriction on working hours. The argument behind this proposition was that freedom of contract and private property were constitutionally protected and if courts permitted a universal abridgement of contract then the guarantees of the due process and contract clauses would not be very far-reaching. In 1905 Mr Justice Peckham made this point:

> It is also urged . . . that . . . therefore any legislation which may be said to tend to make people healthy must be valid as health laws, enacted under the police power. If this is a valid argument . . . it follows that the protection of the Federal Constitution from undue interference with liberty of person and freedom of contract is visionary. . . . Scarcely any law . . . as well as contract, would come under the restrictive sway of the legislature.[38]

As a consequence the courts demanded that if working hours were to be controlled then the legislature must determine that the health of employees was being impaired and furthermore that there must be a reasonable basis for the legislature's belief. Thus the stages of the courts' reasoning process can be summarised in the following manner. Firstly, the protection afforded by the contract and due process clauses is not absolute. Secondly, as a consequence working conditions, including maximum hours legislation, could be regulated by government under its police power. Thirdly, legislation of this type was a legitimate exercise of the police power if it was a reasonable exercise of that power, i.e. if there was a reasonable foundation for the legislature's contention that the health of a particular section of the population was being endangered by working an excessive number of hours. Inevitably it was the definition of reasonableness that was the principal bone

23

of contention in the successive cases that came before the courts. In the *Lochner* case, the Supreme Court found the state of New York had used the police power unreasonably. The legislation which sought to limit the hours worked by bakers did not strike the majority of justices as reasonable, i.e. there were no reasonable grounds to believe that employment of over sixty hours a week in a bakery constituted a health hazard over and above that of any other occupation. However, in *Holden* v. *Hardy*,[39] the Supreme Court sustained the determination of the Utah legislature that there was a danger to the health of miners, a danger distinguishable from most other occupations, and that consequently the state of Utah acted reasonably when it limited the working day to eight hours bar emergencies. But the most interesting case was *Muller* v. *Oregon*[40] which came before the Supreme Court in 1908. Here the Court unanimously upheld the constitutionality of an Oregon law which established a maximum of ten hours per day for women in all industrial occupations. There are three notable characteristics about *Muller*. Firstly, the Court did not adopt its usual position that as all employment is injurious government could only intervene in those industries where the health hazard was above the norm. Instead the nine justices accepted that all industrial occupations posed a serious health hazard. Secondly, the Court was persuaded of this by the nature of the evidence presented to it by counsel for the appellants, Louis Brandeis. Brandeis had included in his brief both medical and sociological data which he believed sustained the validity of this assertion. Thirdly, despite this apparent reversal of its position in earlier cases, the Supreme Court did not in fact change its approach in *Muller* to determining the constitutionality of maximum hours legislation. The question still revolved around the reasonableness of the legislature's belief. Admittedly in *Lochner* the state of New York was thought to be unreasonable while the more far-reaching contention of the Oregon statute was deemed to be reasonable. The explanation for the difference, however, cannot be located in personnel changes, for there had been scant change – both the 'arch-conservatives', Peckham and Brewer, were still on the Court – but in the type of material that was presented to the Court as evidence in the Brandeis brief. Therein lies the reason for the 'switch'. Thus the important point to stress is that the test of reasonableness was not a subterfuge. It was not a guise for striking down legislation in order to support the interests of a property-owning class. The Supreme Court was genuinely amenable to persuasion, it was willing to give credence to the legislature's judgement and the unanimous decision in *Muller* is testimony to that.[41]

Although it is difficult even from this brief resumé of cases concerning rate regulation and maximum hour limitations to sustain the conclusion of Fine, Miller *et al.* that the Supreme Court was reading its own *laissez-faire* beliefs into the Constitution, one can in part understand why they arrive at such a conclusion. There is an ideological flavour about the opinions. The rhetoric of Social Darwinism is present in the *obiter dicta* and certainly one does have the feeling that the high bench had its heart on the right. But it is easy and misleading to be beguiled by the surface verbiage. Indeed, the striking and interesting fact about these opinions is the juxtaposition of the language of ideology and the pragmatic problem-solving attitude present in the reasoning process. Despite the visibility of the rhetoric, it is of course the process of argument and reasoning that is the core of a judicial decision. It is this pragmatic core which contradicts the ideological interpretation of judicial history in the post-Civil War period. As Loren Beth has noted, 'the Court was not, despite some of its critics, wholeheartedly pro-business or pro-free enterprise at any time. Indeed the cases are marked by hesitance, ambiguity, indecisiveness and inconsistency, and in fact many more of its decisions favoured the state than the other way around.'[42]

It is a pity that commentators in the early 1930s did not share Beth's assessment, for if they had they would have been far more wary of taking comfort from the Supreme Court's judgements in *Home Building Loan Association* v. *Blaisdell*[43] and *Nebbia* v. *New York*[44] They would have been far more reluctant to see the *Blaisdell* and *Nebbia* decisions as harbingers of the future.

NOTES
1 A. J. Schlesinger, *The Age of Roosevelt*, Vol. 3 (1966), p. 445.
2 *Ibid.*, p. 457. Schlesinger's observations are shared by the other standard histories of the New Deal. 'Like a legislature,' J. M. Burns wrote, 'the Court had

its right, its left and its center. Lined up as a solid phalanx on the right were . . . Van Devanter, an Old Grand Republican . . . McReynolds . . . the most outspoken conservative democrat . . . The main tie binding these men was . . . their common belief in the ideology of *laissez faire*, individualism and free competition. On the left was a remarkable trio . . . Brandeis, the 'Peoples Advocate' . . . Stone . . . dean of Columbia Law School . . . and Cardozo a brilliant New York State judge . . . In the middle were the 'swingmen' Roberts and Chief Justice Hughes.' J. M. Burns, *Roosevelt: The Lion and the Fox* (1956), p. 230. See also, W. E. Leuchtenburg, *Franklin D. Roosevelt and the New Deal, 1932–40* (1963); 'The origins of Franklin D. Roosevelt's 'Court-Packing' plan' in *The Supreme Court Review*, 1966 (1967); D. Perkins, *The New Age of Franklin Roosevelt* (1956). A similar point of view is to be found in the biographies of the judges who served on the Supreme Court in the 1930s. S. Hendel, *Charles Evans Hughes and the Supreme Court* (1951); S. J. Konefsky, *Chief Justice Stone and the Supreme Court* (1945); C. A. Leonard, 12*A Search for Judicial Philosophy: Mr Justice Roberts and the Constitutional Revolution of 1937* (1971); A. T. Mason, *Brandeis: A Free Man's Life* (1946); Harlan F. Stone: *Pillar of the Law* (1956); J. F. Pascal, *Mr Justice Sutherland: A Man against the State* (1951); M. Pusey, *Charles Evans Hughes* (1952). Essentially the same point of view is found in the few judicial histories of the period, such as E. Erikson, *Supreme Court and the New Deal* (1941); R. H. Jackson, *The Struggle for Judicial Supremacy* (1955); and indeed in the remarkable few scholarly articles of the period. See, in particular, A. T. Mason, 'The conservative world of Mr. Justice Sutherland, 1883–1910', 32 *American Political Science Review* 443 (1938); R. F. Howell, 'The judicial conservatives three decades ago: aristocratic guardians of the prerogatives of property and the judiciary', 4 *Virginia Law Review*, p. 1447 (1962).

3 D. Pearson and R. Allen, *The Nine Old Men* (1937). Van Devanter who was reputed to have been slow and senile has been, in recent years, portrayed rather more favourably. His earlier reputation was based on his 'pen paralysis' and the consequent fact that he rarely wrote an opinion. But apparently his contributions in conference were always lucid, intelligent and he radiated, in the words of Chief Justice Hughes, 'perspicacity and common sense'. See P. A. Freund, 'Charles Evan Hughes as Chief Justice', 81 *Harvard Law Review*, 4, 16.

4 Jackson, *The Struggle for Judicial Supremacy*, p. 175.

5 *Morehead* v. *New York ex rel Tipaldo*, 298 US 587 (1936)

6 A. T. Mason, *The Supreme Court from Taft to Warren* (1964), p. 92.

7 R. G. McCloskey, 'Economic due process and the Supreme Court: an exhumation and reburial' in L. Levy (ed.), *American Constitutional Law* (1966), p. 168.

8 J. F. Paschal, 'Mr Justice Sutherland' in A. Durham and P. Kurland (eds.), *Mr Justice* (1956), p. 203.

9 F. Rodell, *Nine Men: A Political History of the Supreme Court of the United States from 1790 to 1955* (1955), pp. 217, 221, 224, 225.

10 C. H. Pritchett, *The Roosevelt Court: A Study in Judicial Politics and Values 1937–1947* (1969), pp. 3, 19.

11 G. Schubert, *Constitutional Politics* (1964), p. 161.

12 *Ibid.*, p. 165.

13 See F. Frankfurter, 'Mr Justice Roberts', 104 *University of Pennsylvania Law Review*, 313 (1955). Frankfurter's article includes a memorandum from Roberts to Frankfurter written on 9 November 1945, which explains Roberts' apparent change in position in *West Coast Hotel* v. *Parrish*, 300 US 379 (1937) from *Moreland* v. *Tipaldo*, 298 US 587 as no change at all, as the issue raised in the two cases were subtly but very positively different. Furthermore, the charge that

Roberts' alleged switch was caused by President Roosevelt's court-packing plan is shown as unfounded. Although the Court's decision was announced on 29 March 1937, after the court-packing plan was unveiled, the judicial conference in fact had been held on 19 December 1936, some two months before the plans had surfaced in public. The delay between the conference and the decision was entirely due to Justice Stone being ill. Roberts' memorandum is reprinted in M. Freedman (ed.), *Roosevelt and Frankfurter: Their Correspondence 1928–1945* (1967), pp. 392, 395.

**14** Rodell, *Nine Men*, p. 227.

**15** Mason, *Stone*, p. 370.

**16** Commenting on *Blaisdell* the *New York Herald Tribune* wrote, 'great political significance was attached to the fact that Chief Justice Charles Evans Hughes joined the so-called liberal group of the Court and handed down the majority decision'. *New York Herald Tribune*, 10 January 1934, p. 1. The *New York Times* declared, 'for the present, at any rate, the country will be disposed to say: *Roma dixit causa finita est*'. *New York Times*, 10 January 1934, p. 20.

**17** 290 US 1 (1933).

**18** Indeed during the period the Court struck down two out of five state taxes, Government Bonds – *Schuylkell Trust Co.* v. *Pennsylvania*, 296 US 113 (1935); gasoline sold to Navy – *Groves* v. *Texas*, 298 US 393 (1936).

**19** 290 US 398 (1934).

**20** 291 US 503 (1934).

**21** The Fourteenth Amendment which was adopted in 1868 contained a due process clause which placed restrictions on state governments identical to those which the Fifth Amendment placed on the federal government. This litigation concerning constitutional propriety of state economic regulation grew substantially after 1868 and particularly after 1873 and the *Slaughterhouse Cases*, 16 Wall. 36 (1873). The question over the definition of the word 'persons' and the so-called 'Conspiracy Theory' have been dealt with in H. J. Graham, *Everyman's Constitution: Historical Essays on the Fourteenth Amendment, the 'Conspiracy Theory' and American Constitutionalism* (1968), pp. 367–437. See also J. B. James, *The Framing of the Fourteenth Amendment* (1956). A useful reminder that the judiciary were not simply a gullible receptacle for Roscoe Conkling's claims over the framing of the Fourteenth Amendment can be found in C. P. Magrath, *Morrison R. Waite: The Triumph of Character* (1963). Magrath demonstrates that the explicit decision by the Waite Court to include corporations in their definition of person in *Santa Clara County* v. *Southern Pacific Railway Co.*, 118 US 394 (1886), had much more to do with extant judicial practice than with Conkling's testimony before the bench. See Magrath, *Morrison R. Waite*, p. 222–4.

**22** For minimum wage bills, see *Stetler* v. *O'Hara*, 243 US 649 (1917); for hours regulation *Holden* v. *Hardy*, 169 US 366 (1898); and for price regulation see *The Granger Cases* and in particular *Munn* v. *Illinois*, 94 US 113 (1877).

**23** The constitutionality of the income tax law of 1904 was resolved in *Pollock* v. *Farmers Loan and Trust Co.*, 157 US 429 (1895), 158 US 601 (1895). The fate of the Child Labor Tax Law was finally decided in *Bailey* v. *Drexel Furniture Co.*, 259 US 20 (1922).

**24** A. S. Miller, *The Supreme Court and American Capitalism* (1968), pp. 50–1.

**25** S. Fine, *Laissez Faire and the General Welfare State* (1956), p. 126. For essentially the same point of view see R. G. McCloskey, *American Conservatism in the Age of Enterprise* (1951); A. M. Paul, *Conservative Crisis and the Rule of Law* (1969); B. Schwartz, *American Constitutional Law* (1955); C. B. Swisher, *Growth of Constitutional Power in the United States* (1946); B. Twiss, *Lawyers and the Constitution* (1942).

26 W. Letwin, *A Documentary History of American Economic Policy* (1961), pp. xxix–xxx.
27 See *United States* v. *Insurance Companies*, 22 Wall. 99 (1874); *Peck* v. *C & N.W.R. Co.*, 94 US 164 (1877); *Railroad Co.* v. *Richmond*, 96 US 521 (1878).
28 The License Cases, 1 5 How. 504 (1847). Chief Justice Shaw of Massachusetts in another famous definition of the police power wrote, 'the power vested in the legislature by the constitution to make, ordain and establish all manner of wholesome and reasonable laws, statutes and ordinances . . . as they shall judge to be for the good and welfare of the commonwealth and of the subjects of the same.' *Commonwealth* v. *Alger*, 61 Mass. (7 Cush) 53 (1851). See also B. Schwartz, *A Commentary on the Constitution of the United States*, Vol. 2 (1964), passim.
29 *Adkins* v. *Children's Hospital*, 261 US 525, 546 (1923).
30 198 US 45 (1905)
31 *Ibid.*, p. 57.
32 94 US 113 (1876)
33 See Holmes' impassioned dissent in the Lochner case, 198 US 45, 74–6 (1905).
34 *Stone* v. *Farmers' Loan and Trust Co.*, 116 US 307, 331 (1886).
35 *Smyth* v. *Ames*, 169 US 466, 547 (1898).
36 134 US 418 (1890).
37 A. E. Sutherland, *Constitutionalism in America* (1965), p. 463.
38 *Lochner* v. *New York*, 198 US 45, 60 (1905).
39 169 US 366 (1898).
40 208 US 412 (1908).
41 See also *Bunting* v. *Oregon*, 243 US 426 (1917). The Court was more closely divided in Bunting partly because that statute, enacted in 1913, limited the hours of work to ten a day, but it also included a proviso that three additional hours might be worked as overtime at a wage rate 50 per cent higher than normal.
42 L. E. Beth, *The Development of the American Constitution, 1877–1917*, (1971), p. 190.
43 290 US 398 (1934).
44 291 US 502 (1934).

## 3

# Portents for the future: *Home Building and Loan Association* v. *Blaisdell* and *Nebbia* v. *New York*

## I

On 18 April 1933 the Minnesota Mortgage Moratorium Law came into effect.[1] The preamble to the law stated the legislators' belief that the:

> severe financial and economic depression ... has resulted in extremely low prices for the products of the farms and the factories, a great amount of unemployment, an almost complete lack of credit for farmers, businessmen and property owners ... who [are and] will for some time be unable to meet all payments as they come due of ... interest and principal of mortgages on their properties and are, therefore, threatened with loss of such properties through mortgage foreclosures ... the Legislature of Minnesota hereby declares its belief that the conditions existing ... have created an emergency of such nature that justifies and validates legislation for the extension of the time of redemption from mortgage foreclosure ... The State of Minnesota possesses the right under its police power to declare a state of emergency to exist and the inherent and fundamental purpose of our government is to safeguard the public and promote the general welfare of the people.[2]

In order to fulfil these intentions the legislature delineated various forms of relief that could prevent foreclosure. The mode of relief in contention in this case authorised the District Court of the County to extend the period of redemption from foreclosure sales 'for such additional time as the court may deem just and equitable'. However, the District Court also had to determine the 'reasonable value of the income of the property involved in the sale, or if it had no income, then the reasonable value of the property, and [direct] the mortgagor to pay all or a reasonable part of such income or rental value in or toward the payment of taxes, insurance, interest, mortgage'.[3]

The details of the case will perhaps illustrate the manner in which the Mortgage Moratorium Law functioned. John H. Blaisdell and his wife owned a lot in Minneapolis which was mortgaged to the Home Building and Loan Association. They had then defaulted on their payments and the mortgage had been foreclosed. At a foreclosure sale in May 1932, the Association had bought the Blaisdells' property for $3,700.98, which was the amount outstanding on the mortgage. Under the laws of Minnesota that were in effect at the time, the Blaisdells had a year in which they could redeem their property, but they were unable to do so. Consequently they applied to the District Court for the relief provided under the Mortgage Moratorium Law. This they were granted. The court extended the period of redemption by a further two years to May 1935, but the Blaisdells were required to pay to the Association a sum of $40 a month. The Home Building and Loan Association appealed this judgement to the Supreme Court of Minnesota, where the decision of the District Court was upheld. 4 Thereupon the Association appealed to the United States Supreme Court.

On 8 January 1934, the Supreme Court announced its decision. Hughes, speaking for five members of the High Bench, sustained the constitutionality of the Mortgage Moratorium Law. He accepted the State of Minnesota's contention that the law was valid for the reasons it suggested. Firstly, that there was a economic slump in Minnesota. 5 Secondly, that a state, under its police power, has the right to declare an emergency in these economic conditions. Furthermore that for the duration of such an emergency a state has the right to make laws for the benefit and welfare of its citizens. Thirdly, the State of Minnesota had decided to alleviate just one aspect of the hardship caused by the depression – the danger of foreclosure. And, fourthly, it had done so without confiscating private property or using private property without remuneration. It had merely modified the contract between mortgagor and mortgagee, while insisting that the mortgagor maintained a level of repayment during the period of extended redemption. Thus the Attorney-General of Minnesota argued that the Mortgage Moratorium Law was constitutional. But Hughes, while agreeing with this process of reasoning, recognised that the matter could not be resolved quite that easily. The principal objection to the constitutionality of the Moratorium Law, raised by the appellants, was that it abrogated the contract clause. The contract clause says quite specifically that, 'No State shall ... pass any ... law impairing the obligation of contracts.'[6] Now, of course, it had never been assumed that all contracts were sacrosanct or inviolate. Statutes which had prevented lotteries or limited the number of hours that could be worked by women or children had the effect of impairing pre-existing contracts, but the courts had never accepted any claim that these laws were unconstitutional because the contract clause had been violated. For if they had the courts would, in effect, have nullified the police power of government. The judiciary therefore accepted that contracts could be impaired without violating the contract clause. However, this did not mean that the courts were granting the legislative authority an unrestricted power over contractual obligations. For if they did then the contract clause would be meaningless and its protections non-existent. So the limitation that the courts imposed was that a contract could be breached by the state so long as the impairment of contract was the incidental result of a generic governmental regulation. Thus if a legislature made a particular practice illegal, then contracts formulated when the practice was legal could constitutionally be made void. As Mr Justice Sutherland declared, contracts are 'made upon an implied condition that a particular state of things shall continue to exist ... [but] when the state of things ceases to exist, the bargain itself ceases to exist'.[7] However, the judiciary were reluctant to condone a direct abridgement of contract. Judges were wary of validating a statute where the intention was not to modify the social context in which a contract was made, but to modify the contract itself: where the lawfulness of the contract, either at the time of adjudication or at the point it was extended into, was not being challenged, but its enforcement was being hindered. It had been assumed until then that the contract clause would be a constitutional impediment to any such legislative activity. Thus this was the problem that faced the Chief Justice. For the Mortgage Moratorium Law was specifically intended to modify existing contracts. There was no claim by the state that the contract between Blaisdell and the Association was unlawful at any time; there was no attempt to suggest that this statute was intended to change public or private mores which then had a consequential effect on the contractual obligations between mortgagor and mortgagee. The *raison d'être* of this statute was to amend contractual obligations which were still lawful and had been voluntarily entered into by two private parties.

Chief Justice Hughes had a formidable task on his hands, if he wished to formulate a reasoned and persuasive argument on behalf of the statute's constitutionality. His opinion which succeeds in doing precisely that is testimony to his subtle and sophisticated judicial mind. For the hurdles he had to overcome were very substantial indeed. Two of the principal elements in constitutional adjudication, the intent of the Founding Fathers and earlier judicial interpretations of the Constitution, did not give Hughes very much help. Both Hughes and Sutherland, who wrote the dissent, were agreed on the historical context of the contract clause,[8] that the contract clause was formulated in response to events that occurred in the various states during the period of Confederation. According to Hughes:

> the reasons which led to adoption of that [contract] clause . . . are not left in doubt . . . The widespread distress following the revolutionary period and the plight of the debtors had called forth in the States an ignoble array of legislative schemes for the defeat of creditors and the invasion of contractual obligations. Legislative interferences had been so numerous and extreme that the confidence essential to prosperous trade had been undermined and the utter destruction of credit was threatened.[9]

He goes on to quote, with approval, Chief Justice Marshall in *Ogden* v. *Saunders*:

> The power of changing the relative situation of debtor and creditor, of interfering with contracts, . . . had been used to such an excess by the state legislatures, as to break upon the ordinary intercourse of society . . . The mischief had become so great as to . . . threaten the existence of credit . . . and the morals of the people. *To guard against the continuance of the evil was an object of deep interest . . . and was one of the important benefits expected from the reform of the government.*[10]

Sutherland agreed with and reinforced Hughes' interpretation of history and furthermore proceeded to chronicle the evidence which demonstrated that the Framers were aware of the kind of legislative practices mentioned by Hughes, and condemned them, and that Article 1, Section 10 was specifically included in the Constitution to prevent such actions.[11] But, of course, this understanding of the emergence of the contract clause tended to support Sutherland's position fairly strongly. There appeared to be a close parallel between the conditions during the period of Confederation and those of the Great Depression. And despite the economic hardship suffered during the Confederation the Founding Fathers appear to have taken exception to legislative attempts to alleviate distress by modifying contractual obligations, and thereupon devised the contract clause to prevent any similar practices recurring. The Minnesota legislation tended to have an unfortunate resemblance to these earlier modes of legislative relief, which had aroused the Framers' disapproval. However, the verdict in this case could not be decided merely on constitutional intent. For the Framers could not possibly conceive of the myriad of circumstances and conflicts that could and did arise. And so inevitably it would be up to the judiciary to interpret the meaning of the contract clause in the 150 years that had elapsed since the Federal Constitutional Convention.

Unfortunately the earlier rulings of the Supreme Court also did not provide much comfort for Hughes, although the legal position was somewhat confused. As mentioned above, the contract clause had been interpreted to allow states to break private contractual obligations as long as it was part and parcel of a wider regulation. The case which appeared to be controlling was *Bronson* v. *Kinzie*.[12] The facts in *Bronson* were similar to *Blaisdell*. In 1841 the Illinois legislature had passed two statutes, admittedly without declaring an emergency, with the intent of amending existing contracts. Under these laws the period of redemption for the mortgage was extended by one year. Furthermore any sale, which resulted from a foreclosure, was prevented unless the sum bid amounted to two-thirds of the property's appraisal value. In 1843, the Supreme Court, speaking through Chief Justice Taney, declared the Illinois legislation unconstitutional. Taney appeared to close most loopholes, when he declared:

> The law gives to the mortgagor ... an equitable estate in the premises which ... [he would not have been entitled to under the original contract, and this new interest ... is directly and materially in conflict with those which the mortgagee acquired when the mortgage was made. *Any such modification of a contract by subsequent legislation against the consent of one of the parties, unquestionably impairs its obligation and is prohibited by the Constitution.*[13]

Subsequently the Supreme Court accepted and enforced Taney's interpretation of the contract clause and its obligations. For example, in *Barnitz* v. *Beverly*,[14] the Court made void a Kansas statute which authorised either the redemption of property, where no previous right had existed contractually, or an extension to the period of redemption. Similarly in *Howard* v. *Bugbee*,[15] the Court held that an Alabama law, which amended contractual obligations by permitting the redemption of mortgages within two years after foreclosure sale, was unconstitutional under the *Bronson* rule.[16] Thus the Court gave the impression that it would not, after *Bronson*, permit a direct abridgement of contract.

However, in the Rent Cases there was an apparent deviation from the *Bronson* rule. In three cases which came before the Supreme Court in 1921 and 1922, the Court by the narrowest of majorities sustained the constitutionality of two laws which directly amended contractual obligations. In *Block* v. *Hirsh*[17] the Supreme Court upheld an Act of Congress affecting the District of Columbia which authorised tenants to remain in occupation of rented apartments even though their lease had expired. Of course as the contract clause does not restrict the powers of the federal government, this case was not strictly germane to a discussion of the contract clause. But in the other two cases, *Marcus Brown Holding Co.* v. *Feldman*[18] and *Levi Leading Co.* v. *Siegel*,[19] the Court validated very similar state laws. In 1920 the state of New York declared that a public emergency existed and thereupon passed laws which deprived the owners of rented accommodation of their rights of repossessing their property from those tenants who were occupying the premises as long as those tenants were prepared to pay a reasonable rent for the accommodation. This suspension of the owner's right of repossession was to last for two years until November 1922. There is little doubt that the New York law 'directly interfered with the enforcement of convenants'[20] But Mr Justice Holmes' opinion in *Marcus Brown* did not attempt to deal with the question of contract impairment. In a very short opinion, only three pages long, Holmes devoted a mere paragraph to this problem. Instead he relied heavily on his own earlier opinion in *Block* v. *Hirsh* and concluded:

> The earlier objections to these acts [the New York statutes] have been dealt with in *Block* v. *Hirsh*. In the present case more emphasis is laid upon the impairment of the obligation of the contract . . . But contracts are made subject to this exercise of the power of the State when otherwise justified, as we have held this to be.[21]

Thus Holmes did not really come to terms with the awkward issues of contractual impairment. But he had, in effect, overruled *Bronson*. Holmes had based his judgement on the inherent power of the State of New York to declare an emergency on the fact that the regulation was of a temporary kind and that there was reasonable compensation for the landlord during the interregnum – precisely the same kind of reasoning used by the State of Minnesota in favour of its Mortgage Moratorium Law. Yet curiously Hughes did not rely on Holmes' opinion. Samuel Hendel believes that in not doing so, Hughes made a mistake. 'Had he [Hughes] chosen to predicate his decision on that basis [the rent cases] . . . there would have been little basis for objection.'[22] So an interesting question arises as to why the Chief Justice did not use the Holmes formula in *Blaisdell*. The answer could not be that he was unaware of the solution available in the Rent Cases. The parallel between the Minnesota legislation and the New York laws, with reference to contractual obligations, was striking and inescapable. Despite this, Hughes chose to travel a more circuitous and tenuous route, thereby opening avenues for criticism which would otherwise have remained closed.

The Chief Justice decided to base the defence of his assessment that the Minnesota law was constitutional on the notion of emergency. He used the war power of the federal government as a simile. 'While emergency does not create power, emergency may furnish the occasion for the exercise of that power.'[23] This is another way of saying that while the occurrence of war does not create the war power, it is only during a war that the war power may be used. Thus, drawing on this simile, Hughes claimed that there were powers inherent in a state which could be used only in a state of emergency.

> But it does not follow that conditions may not arise in which a temporary restraint of enforcement may be consistent with the spirit and purpose of the . . . [contract clause] and thus be found to be within the range of the reserved power of the State to protect the vital interests of the community. It cannot be maintained that the constitutional prohibition should be so constrained as to prevent limited and temporary interpositions with respect to the enforcement of contracts if made necessary by a great public calamity such as fire, flood or earthquake . . . The reservation of state power appropriate to such extraordinary conditions may be deemed to be as much a part of all contracts, as is the reservation of state power to protect the public interest in the other situations to which we have referred. And if state power exists to give temporary relief from the enforcement of contracts in the presence of disasters due to physical causes . . . that power cannot be said to be non-existent when the urgent public need demanding such relief is produced by other and economic means.[24]

This, then, was the intellectual core of Hughes' opinion; emergency, or rather the conditions causing a state of emergency, justified the Minnesota law. Admittedly there were certain other subordinate requirements: namely that private property was not being confiscated or used without reasonable compensation; that the regulation 'was addressed to a legitimate end . . . and was not for the mere advantage of particular individuals but for the protection of the basic interest in society'.[25] The Mortgage Moratorium Law fulfilled these conditions. But the critical test of constitutionality for this statute was whether conditions for a state of emergency prevailed in Minnesota. Here the Chief Justice accepted both the legislature's, and more importantly the Supreme Court of Minnesota's view that there were grounds for declaring an emergency to exist. Thus the Mortgage Moratorium Law was constitutional.

When Hughes circulated his opinion amongst his brethren,

Mr Justice Brandeis wrote on his proof sheets: 'Yes. Strongly put and interesting. I approve of the changes proposed.'[26] But Brandeis's approval was not shared by two other members of the majority, Justices Cardozo and Stone. Cardozo, in fact, drafted a concurring opinion and Stone submitted a memorandum to the Chief Justice outlining his position.[27] However his disagreement never came into the open because Hughes was able to convince his brethren, through a combination of persuasion and compromise, not to fragment the majority.[28] Nevertheless it is not difficult to understand Cardozo's and Stone's uneasiness with the Chief Justice's opinion. Hughes had made it vulnerable to attack by constructing the opinion on the foundation of emergency. Sutherland, who had an acute eye for weakness, homed in on the parallel Hughes had drawn with the war power of the federal government. With an irony bordering on scorn, Sutherland declared:

> The opinion concedes that emergency does not create power, or increase granted power, or remove or diminish restrictions upon power granted or reserved. It then proceeds to say, however, that while emergency does not create power it may furnish the occasion for the exercise of power. I can only interpret what is said on the subject as meaning that while an emergency does not diminish a restriction upon power it furnishes an occasion for diminishing it; and this, as it seems to me, is merely the same thing by the use of another set of words with the effect of affirming that which has just be denied.'[29]

But while Sutherland was able to expose the fragility of Hughes' rather tortured analogical reasoning, he did not fatally damage the Chief Justice's opinion. And clearly Hughes was prepared to pay the price of Sutherland's acid remarks. For he could have avoided them by adopting Holmes' examples of simply putting aside the issue of contractual obligations or by accepting the advice of Stone's memorandum, which claimed that the unprecedented economic problems the nation faced demanded unprecedented solutions.[30] But Hughes chose not to do so.

The attractions, at least to Hughes, of erecting his opinion on the rather frail foundations of emergency powers were manifold. Firstly, and although it may at first glance appear perverse,

Hughes was able to reassert that the restrictions imposed on the state by the contract clause were still meaningful. For he made it clear that, apart from emergencies, Article 1, Section 10 still prevented amendments to contracts by state governments as defined in *Bronson*. This re-established the position that existed prior to the Rent Cases and before Holmes' cursory and brusque dismissal of the protections afforded by the contract clause. This presumably was the reason why Hughes did not rely on the Rent Cases. One suspects that he, as well as Sutherland, was unhappy with *Marcus Brown*, if not with the content, then certainly with its style and mode of reasoning.[31] Thus he wanted to restore the protections of the contract clause from the constitutional shadow they had fallen under in the Rent Cases. The Chief Justice realised he could do this and also find the Moratorium Law constitutional under the umbrella of emergency powers. Secondly, the umbrella was not a very large one, for emergencies by definition are temporary conditions. They are an aberration: a period of extraordinary events. As soon as conditions return to normal emergency powers lapse. Thirdly, there was no basis to fear that the use of emergency powers in *Blaisdell* was the thin end of the wedge. For Hughes took considerable care to forestall any possible future attempt by legislatures to abuse emergency powers. He claimed that courts had the authority to scrutinise every legislative declaration of emergency and that judges, not legislators, would be the final arbiters in this matter: 'while the declaration by the legislature as to the existence of the emergency was entitled to great respect, it was not conclusive; . . . *It is always open to judicial enquiry whether the exigency still exists upon which the continued operation of the law depends.*'[32]

Thus the advantages of making the concept of emergency powers the fulcrum of the opinion are apparent. It permitted the Chief Justice to uphold the Mortgage Moratorium Law, but it allowed him to do so without creating a new and major grant of power to the state government. The emergency power that was granted was circumscribed by time and events and furthermore remained under judicial supervision. It also allowed Hughes to reassess the constitutional importance of the contract clause with its traditional ramifications. Therefore it gave Hughes the opportunity, at one and the same time to accede to governmental intervention in the economy, but without substantially lessening any of the constitutional restrictions on the legislative power. Nor did *Blaisdell* provide for any further weakening of these limitations. Sutherland misconstrued the majority opinion when he claimed that: 'Few questions of greater moment than that just decided have been submitted for judicial enquiry this generation. He simply closes his eyes to the necessary implications of the decision who fails to see in it the potentiality of . . . serious and dangerous inroads upon the limitation of the Constitution which are almost certain to ensue.'[33] Hughes was not endangering the Constitution. Both Hughes and Sutherland shared the same objective; the protection of private property and contractual obligations as constitutional imperatives. Possibly Sutherland was misled by Hughes' occasional forays into gradiloquent rhetoric: 'We must never forget that it is a constitution we are expounding,' wrote Hughes recalling the words of Chief Justice Marshall, 'a constitution intended to endure for ages to come, and, consequently, to be adapted to the various crises of human affairs.'[34] Certainly Merlo Pusey is dazzled by the Hughes *obiter dicta*. Pusey, like Sutherland, believed that *Blaisdell* was a break with the past with portents for the future, but unlike Sutherland Pusey welcomed the judgement: 'It was a narrow victory, for forward-marching constitutionalism. He [Hughes] spoke . . . the language that was on the lips of legislators, editors and leaders of the Roosevelt administration.'[35]

One can understand Sutherland's and Pusey's misunderstanding of the opinion. Judges who quoted Marshall's words in *McCulloch* v. *Maryland*[36] or Holmes' in *Missouri* v. *Holland*[37] were usually about to concede a grant of power to legislatures although they were unable to locate the appropriate historical and constitutional basis for doing so. But this was not the case in *Blaisdell* for no substantial new legislative power was being conceded. Indeed these rhetorical excursions read strangely as they are at odds with the structure of the opinion. On the one hand Hughes' language is on occasion dramatic and sweeping, but on the other the structure of argument and reasoning is indisputably cautious and precise. Conceivably Hughes wanted to create the impression of a 'forward-marching constitutionalism'. In this he appears to have been successful.[38] Possibly he wanted to draw attention away from the very limited grounds on which the Minnesota legislation was being sustained. But whatever the reason it was a pity, a pity for several reasons.

Firstly, it drew attention away from the reality of Hughes' opinion which was a very considerable achievement. The opinion was a brilliantly orchestrated piece of creative judicial writing in the common law tradition. Hughes' argument was subtle, intelligent and used precedent rather than being imprisoned by it. This enabled him to fulfil his objective of finding the Moratorium Law constitutional without rewriting constitutional history. He was able to permit the law to stand without destroying the credibility of the contract clause and its protections as well as preserving the integrity of prior judicial interpretations, bar the Rent Cases, of the clause. This then was the measure of the Chief Justice's achievement and it ought to be recognised rather than caricatured. But secondly, the opinion did also create a false sense of expectation, a sense which was based on the belief that the 'liberals' on the Court were now in control and that they would sustain the validity of the Roosevelt administration's varied interventions in the economy. But this belief was based on an inaccurate analysis of *Blaisdell* and the expectations aroused were doomed to frustration.[39]

### II

Less than two months after *Blaisdell*, on 5 March 1934, the Supreme Court announced its opinion in *Nebbia* v. *New York*[40] The central issue in this case was the constitutionality of the Milk Control Law, which the New York legislature had passed in 1933.[41] The Milk Control Law was, in the words of the New York State brief, 'designed and enacted for the purpose of regulating the price of milk in the State of New York.'[42] The legislature had embarked on such a course of action because of the severity of the depression in the farming community. 'In the four years from March 1929 to March 1933, the retail price of milk fell 37%, but the price paid to the farmers fell 61%.'[43] In their search for a remedy to this severe problem, the Senate and Assembly of New York created a joint legislative committee to examine the situation pertaining to the production, distribution and retailing of milk. After an extremely thorough investigation lasting about a year this committee concluded that the operation of market forces would not resolve the economic problems of the dairy industry during the depression. Therefore, the committee urged the legislature to regulate the industry by establishing a minimum and maximum price for milk in order to resolve the crisis. The legislature accepted this recommendation and on 10 April 1933, the Milk Control Law came into effect.

In order to fulfil the intentions behind the law, a Milk Control Board was established. The Board had the power to supervise and regulate the milk industry over a host of matters; but its significant grant of power was contained in Section 312, subsections A and B of the Act. 'The board shall ascertain . . . what prices for milk . . . will best protect the milk industry in the state . . . and be most in the public interest . . . After such investigation the board shall by official order fix the maximum and minimum wholesale and retail prices to be charged by milk dealers.'[44] The Board under this authority decided that, in the public interest and in the interest of restoring profitability to the dairy industry, a minimum retail price of 9 cents a quart was necessary. However, one Leo Nebbia, who owned a grocery in Rochester, sold two quarts of milk plus a 5-cent loaf of bread for a total of 18 cents. Nebbia was thereupon prosecuted for violating the Milk Control Law and found guilty. Nebbia appealed his conviction first to the county court and subsequently to the New York Court of Appeals but to no avail. He thereupon took his case to the United States Supreme Court.[45]

The Supreme Court proved to be no more sympathetic to Nebbia's cause. A majority of the Court, the *Blaisdell* majority, dismissed Nebbia's contention that the Milk Control Law was in violation of the due process and equal protection clauses of the Fourteenth Amendment. Counsel for Nebbia argued that the regulations issued by the Milk Control Board had seriously damaged, and perhaps had even put in jeopardy the very existence of Nebbia's business. For instance, Nebbia, who was a 'cash and carry' dealer in milk (i.e. he owned a grocery store and sold milk over the counter) was seriously disadvantaged by the Board's regulations. Nebbia was obliged to sell milk in the store at 9 cents a quart or 5 cents a pint, but a rival who had no store but 'a wagon and delivery route . . . was allowed to sell pints of milk as low as Nebbia, with delivery to the customer's door as a bonus. When delivering a quart of milk, the route dealer had to charge only a cent more than Nebbia, a most inadequate differential.'[46] Apart from treating 'cash and carry' dealers invidiously, counsel for Nebbia, while agreeing with the legislature's assessment that there was a serious imbalance between supply and demand in the industry, argued that the method the Milk Board had chosen to remedy the problem was injurious to their client's interests. 'Obviously some persons, like Nebbia, will not be able to sell at the heightened price, inasmuch as there is an oversupply of milk for sale. To such a dealer the legislature gives the alternative of voluntarily ceasing sales or being obliged to cease under penal sanctions . . .and thus be put out of the milk business.'[47]

Nebbia's livelihood was being threatened and if that was the case, then Nebbia, so it was argued, had a claim for redress particularly under the due process clause. Now the brief was not drawn up by naïve or unsophisticated lawyers.[48] They realised that Nebbia's claim that the Milk Control Law was harmful to his interests would by itself be unpersuasive. The legislature of New York under its police power had the constitutional authority to regulate certain aspects of the State's economic life and if, as a consequence of these legitimate regulations, particular individuals suffered financial hardship, then they would simply have to accept it, as hardship *per se* was not a basis for invalidating the regulations. Thus the crucial question in *Nebbia* was not whether Leo Nebbia was adversely affected by the Milk Control Law but whether the regulations issued by the Board were a reasonable exercise of the police power and, getting to the very crux of the case, whether the State of New York had the constitutional authority to regulate the dairy industry. The only way the latter question could be discussed in 1934 was within the reference that had been initially proposed in *Munn* v. *Illinois*, some fifty-eight years earlier and which had been subsequently modified in the intervening period.[49] Counsel for Nebbia, the majority opinion by Mr Justice Roberts and Mr Justice McReynold's minority opinion were at least in agreement on that.

*Munn* had arisen from the conditions of the agricultural industry after the Civil War:

> The close of the the Civil War brought hardship to farmers. They had experienced great prosperity during the war, but now were faced with reduced demands for their products at the very time when their production was sharply on the increase. As in other major war periods . . . many of them had incurred heavy debts . . . but with the close of the war there began a long . . . downward drift of prices which was not to reach its nadir until 1896.[50]

Between 1865 and 1870 price levels measured by the index of prices had fallen by a quarter.[51] Thus faced with declining commodity prices and the consequences of increased debt, farmers turned, in a hallowed American tradition, to the legislatures for relief. The relief they wanted in particular was a reduction in the cost of railroad freight and in the storage of grain. On the whole legislators were sympathetic and even when they were not, they were fully aware of the political power of farmers. Consequently a series of acts were passed establishing a maximum rate for railroad freight and grain warehousing.[52] In 1871 the Illinois Warehouse Act established such a rate for grain storage and two owners of a Chicago warehouse, Ira Munn and George L. Scott, were found guilty of exceeding the stated level. They appealed their convictions to the Illinois Supreme Court but were unsuccessful. Nor were they any more successful in their appeal to the United States Supreme Court, to the chagrin of the owners of the railroads and grain warehouses who had assembled an awesome array of legal talent to contest the case. In their submissions to the court, the attorneys for Munn and Scott argued that the state legislature had no right to regulate the prices charged by warehouse operators. They suggested that this was beyond the State of Illinois' police powers and that it furthermore violated the guarantees of private property embodied in the due process clause of the Fourteenth Amendment. Munn's and Scott's attorneys also offered a variety of other grounds for declaring the Warehouse Act unconstitutional, but the due process clause and abuse of police powers argument was the heart of their claim. Unfortunately for them Chief Justice Waite's majority opinion took a very different view.

Firstly, Waite quoted Taney's[53] definition of the police power and then embellished it by adding:

> Under these powers the government regulates the conduct of its citizens one towards another, and the manner in which each shall use his own property, when such regulation becomes necessary for the public good. In their exercise it has been customary in England from time immemorial and in this country from its first colonization, to regulate ferries, common carriers, hackmen ... and in so doing to fix a maximum charge to be made ... To this day, statutes are to be found in many of the States upon some or all these subjects; and we think it has never yet been successfully contended that such legislation came within any of the constitutional prohibitions against interference with private property.'[54]

Waite then concluded: 'From this it is apparent that ... it was not supposed that statutes regulating the use ... of private property necessarily deprived an owner of his property without due process of the law. *Under some circumstances they may but not under all.*'[55] Thus Waite took the broad but well-established view of the police power. The government for a long time, Waite argued, had regulated the use of private property including prices without denying due process and therefore could continue to do so. But he qualified this in the last sentence of the above remarks by suggesting that there were circumstances when governmental regulation could well deny due process. What then were these circumstances?

The answer offered by Waite was suggested to him by Mr. Justice Bradley.[56] He urged Waite to read and then use a seventeenth-century treatise entitled *De Portibus Maris* written by Lord Chief Justice Hale. Bradley thought it could provide a basis for distinguishing between the circumstances when due process was violated and when it was not. Waite was receptive and his opinion makes extensive use of Hale's treatise. With evident approval, Waite quoted from *De Portibus Maris*, 'when private property is "affected with a public interest it ceases to be *juris privati* only" '.[57] Waite then expanded on this point in his own words:

> This was said by Lord Chief Justice Hale more than two hundred years ago ... and has been accepted without objection as an

essential element in the law of property ever since. Property does become clothed with a public interest when used in a manner to make it of public consequence ... When ... one devotes his property to a use in which the public has an interest, he, in effect, grants to the public an interest in that use, and must submit to be controlled by the public for the common good ... He may withdraw his grant by discontinuing the use; but, so long as he maintains the use, he must submit to the control.:[58]

Thus property which is affected with the public interest can be regulated in various ways including price control, without a denial of due process. In *Munn*, Waite found that grain warehousing was so affected, therefore the State of Illinois had the right to impose a maximum on the prices that the industry charged for its services. But the reverse of Waite's and Hale's proposition 'that property affected with a public interest ceases to be *juris privati*' is that property which is not so affected is not susceptible to governmental regulation. Waite referred to contracts over which 'the legislature has no control ... because the public has no interest'.[59] But how then does one distinguish between private property and property affected with a public interest? Waite was confident that grain warehousing fell in the latter category. 'Certainly if any business can be clothed with a public interest ... this has been.'[60]

But Waite's confident assertion about grain elevators was really no more than that – an assertion – for he offers remarkably little in the way of guidelines or instructions as to how to categorise industries. Rather, he appears to have been satisfied with the all but tautologous proposition that an industry affected with the public interest is an industry in which the public has an interest: a target far too tempting for the pen of Mr Justice Field who wrote the dissenting opinion in *Munn*:

The public is interested in the manufacture of cotton, woollen, and silken fabrics, in the construction of machinery, in the printing and publication of books and periodicals and in the making of utensils of every variety, useful and ornamental, indeed, there is hardly an enterprise or business engaging the attention and labor of any considerable portion of the community in which the public has not an interest in the sense in which the term is used by the court.'[61]

Undoubtedly, Field was indulging in the freedom offered by a dissenting opinion but nevertheless he does have a very serious point. For if the *munn* majority wanted to create two categories of industry, then there had to be a more explicit line of demarcation between the two than the one being offered by Waite. Otherwise a position could develop where all industries would be deemed to have been affected with a public interest, as Field was suggesting, or conversely where none were. In either event the utility of the public interest concept would be regarded. So the problem for the courts post-*Munn* was to provide, if not a definition, then at least guidelines which could help legislatures and judges to distinguish between industries. Whether courts were successful in doing so in the sixty years after *Munn* is moot.

Merlo Pusey, in his biography of Chief Justice Hughes, claimed that 'Justice Roberts is said to have paced the floor of his home until the early morning hours in the process of deciding which way he would turn.'[62] And one can understand the cause of Roberts' hesitation and doubt. The 'affected with the public interest' rule was controlling in 1934 but the attempts to improve and modify *Munn* in the intervening years had not been an unqualified success. Indeed by 1934, the 'affected with the public interest' doctrine in many respects appeared to have outlived its judicial usefulness. In 1877, Chief Justice Waite and the majority of his brethren saw the opinion of the Court as providing government with a broad grant of power. They did not conceive of this grant as a break with the past or the inception of a radically new extension of governmental authority. In fact, according to Waite's biographer, C. P. Magrath, 'the majority regarded their decision as unexceptional . . . despite its political and economic significance. A decision which would . . . do little more than carry out and give practical effect to the Common Law . . .'.[63] If this indeed was accurate and Waite's intention was to do no more than ratify the common law position then his excursion into legal history was unfortunate. The issues in *Munn* could have been resolved within the framework of the due process clause and the reasonable exercise of the police power without using, or misusing, according to Charles Fairman, *De Portibus Maris*.[64] For the consequence of relying on the Lord Chief Justice Hale's treatise, or rather on

Waite's interpretation of it, was twofold. Firstly, judges felt obliged to work within the framework and started to classify various industries into their 'appropriate' category. Secondly, the 'affected with the public interest' rule was almost inevitably going to develop in a more restrictive manner than originally intended for the following reason. If the assumption was that all industries were not affected with the public interest then judges had to discover distinguishing characteristics which differentiated those which were affected from those which were not. Over the years as judges continued their search for more precise and detailed guidelines they incrementally, slowly but surely, reduced the number of industries that fell within the 'affected with the public interest' class. Particularly in the 1920s, the Supreme Court in a series of cases like *Chas. Wolff Packing Co.* v. *Industrial Court*[65] *Tyson and Bro-United Theatre Ticket Officers* v. *Banton*[66] and *Ribnik* v. *McBride*[67] had concluded that only private monopolies and public utilities were 'affected with public interest'. But this was not what the *Munn* majority had intended. So why had the Supreme Court misinterpreted the spirit of Waite's opinion? It was not, as some have suggested, that the Court was overly sympathetic to business interests.[68] The answer is more likely to be found in the nature of the judicial function. The 'affected with the public interest' rule was simply too vague and too loose to be used as a tool in adjudication. It gave the judiciary no guidance. To put it simply, it needed to be made more precise, more concrete; it needed to identify those characteristics which then would enable judges to carry out the classification of industries. The *Munn* rule unmodified was no help. But as judges 'hardened' the rule for sound and intelligent adjudicatory reasons they also inevitably decreased the extent of its constituency. The two developments were simply the reverse side of the same coin. The result was that by 1934 the Court had a precise rule but one which only applied to a narrow band of industries, which was not Waite's intention or indeed even the pre-*Munn* position. The judicial usefulness of the 'affected with the public interest' rule was open to question and in *Nebbia* Mr Justice Roberts chose to do just that.

If the 'affected with the public interest' rule was applied to the facts in *Nebbia*, then the Milk Control Law undoubtedly would have been held unconstitutional. The issue of monopoly was irrelevant, and as Roberts admitted, the dairy industry was not a public utility: 'We may as well say at once that the dairy industry is not . . . a public utility. We think the appellant is also right in asserting that there is in this case no suggestion of any monopoly or monopolistic practice.'[69] Thus the fate of the Law would have been sealed. But Roberts chose not to apply the rule. He decided instead to evaluate the constitutionality of the Law within the pre-*Munn* reference of due process and the reasonable exercise of the police power. He concluded that the Milk Control Law was indeed a reasonable exercise of the police power and thus did not violate the due process clause. Nebbia's contention of an equal protection violation was easily dismissed. To achieve his conclusion Roberts had to establish four points. Firstly, he had to demonstrate the significance of the dairy industry to the economy and citizens of New York, which was a fairly easy task.

> The production and distribution of milk is a paramount industry of the state and largely affects the health and prosperity of its people. Dairying yields fully one-half of the total income from all farm products. Dairy farm investment amounts to approximately $1,000,000,000. Curtailment or destruction of the dairy industry would cause a serious economic loss to people of the state.'[70]

Furthermore, Roberts was able to point out that the industry had been frequently regulated, if not in terms of prices. 'The milk industry in New York has been the subject of long-standing and drastic regulation in the public interest.'[71] Secondly, over the matter of the police power, Roberts took a broad view again quoting Chief Justice Taney:

> But what are the police powers of a state? They are nothing more or less than the powers of government inherent in every sovereignty to the extent of its dominions. And whether a state passes a quarantine law, or a law to punish offences . . . it exercises the same powers; that is to say the power of sovereignty, the power to govern men and things within the limits of its dominion.[72]

Roberts himself added, 'this court from the early days affirmed that the power to promote the general welfare is inherent in government'.[73] But if Roberts defined the police power broadly, he, of course, did not take the view that it was an uncontrolled power. The were limitations on the exercise of the police power not least in the realm of property, as private property was constitutionally protected. The third element of Roberts' opinion was his view of the protection afforded private property by the Constitution and in particular by the due process clause. Again Roberts' view was well established and sustained by authority: 'Under our form of government the use of property and the making of contracts are normally matters of private and not of public concern. The general rule is that both shall be free of governmental interference. *But neither property rights nor contracts are absolute.*'[74] But if the property rights are not absolute, in what form and to what extent do the due process clauses of the Fifth and Fourteenth Amendments offer protection?

> The Fifth Amendment, in the field of federal activity and the Fourteenth as respects state action do not prohibit governmental regulation for the public welfare. They . . . condition the exertion of the admitted power, by securing that the end shall be accomplished by methods consistent with due process. And the guaranty of due process as has often been held, demands that the law shall not be unreasonable, arbitrary or capricious, and that the means selected shall have a real and substantial relation to the object sought to be attained.[75]

Thus the fourth and final point of Roberts' opinion was reached with the question, was the Milk Control Law unreasonable and arbitrary? Roberts responded: 'Tested by these considerations [of being arbitrary and unreasonable] we find no basis in the due process clause of the Fourteenth Amendment for condemning the provisions of the Law here drawn into question.'[76] Thus the Milk Control Law was constitutional.

Roberts' opinion can be summarised in the following manner. The balance between the police power and the due process protections is very fine and delicate. It is therefore up to the judiciary to ensure that the constitutionally guaranteed protections are maintained but without unnecessarily limiting governmental authority. To achieve this balance the courts had always permitted government a considerable latitude as long as they used their power reasonably and without caprice. There was, the *Nebbia* majority concluded, no evidence from the Milk Control Law to suggest that the New York legislature had behaved arbitrarily and unreasonably. Thus the legislation was constitutional. But Roberts simply could not let the argument rest there. After all, what had happened to the 'affected with the public interest' rule? Roberts was burying it, but at least he was doing so openly and with a decency that had been absent from the Court on other occasions.[77]

> In several of the decisions of this court wherein the expression 'affected with a public interest' and 'clothed with a public use' have been brought forward as the criterion of the validity of price control, *it has been admitted that they are not susceptible of definition and form an unsatisfactory test of the constitutionality of legislation directed at business practices or prices.*[78]

But why did Roberts discard the rule? Principally for the reasons mentioned above; the rule had outlived its usefulness and in the common law tradition such a rule ought to be discarded. Governing rules do and indeed must change. Rules which are formulated to cope with given facts may no longer be appropriate for subsequent developments. Again a rule, after a period of time, may be so riddled with exceptions that it no longer continues to be a useful weapon in the judicial armoury. Similarly, a rule formulated to resolve a particular legal dispute may after a period of years be modified and changed in such a manner that it no longer fulfils its original function. That is what happened with the 'affected with the public interest' rule, it became too restrictive and Roberts properly discarded it. But the rule with which he replaced it did not change the balance between governmental power and constitutional restrictions; it did not authorise any new power or offer a greater freedom to the use of existing powers to government. Rather, Roberts was reinstating a rule with a long, established and well, practised formula for evaluating the issue of governmental regulation of prices. The dissenting opinion of Mr Justice McReynolds rather obstinately refused to recognise this. In his desire to retain the 'affected with the public interest' rule, McReynolds angrily but correctly realised that it was being discarded. '*Munn* v. *Illinois* has been much discussed in the opinions referred to above. And always the conclusion was that nothing there sustains the notion that the ordinary business of dealing in commodities is charged with a public interest and subject to legislative control. *The contrary has been distinctly announced.*'[79] But his subsequent charge, that Roberts' opinion was the first step on the road to the 'destruction . . . of the Constitution. Then, all rights will be subject to the ]caprice of the hour . . .'[80] was misplaced. Roberts was not removing or lessening the Constitution's protections of private property. He was not issuing a blank cheque to legislators which would allow them to impose price controls freely and without judicial scrutiny. He carefully and deliberately pointed out that 'Price control is unconstitutional. . . if arbitrary, discriminating or demonstrably irrelevant to the policy the legislative is free to adopt and hence an unnecessary and unwarranted interference with individual liberty.'[81] Roberts continued, even declaring that if price control was 'valid for one sort of business . . . it may be invalid for another sort, or for the same business under other circumstances, because the reasonableness of each regulation depends upon the relevant facts.'[82]

Roberts was not offering politicians a *carte blanche*. But even if McReynolds was unpersuaded by Roberts' words, he should have realised that Roberts was too cautious a jurist and too precise a legal technician to embark on a constitutional revolution. The four years that Roberts had already served on the Supreme Court should have convinced McReynolds that such a charge was absurd. But perhaps it was the very vehemence and extent of McReynolds' charge that convinced observers of the Court that *Nebbia* was a dramatic break with the past. 'As it stands,' wrote the *New Republic*, 'the decision has created the . . . impression that the Supreme Court sees no unconstitutionality in the Roosevelt program.'[83] As with *Blaisdell*, such assessments were unfounded and would make the forthcoming 'defeats' even less palatable.

**NOTES**

1 Chapter 339, *Laws of Minnesota*, 1933.
2 290 US 398 (1934), 421–3.
3 *Ibid.*, pp. 416, 417.
4 189 Minn. 488 (1933).
5 In his submission before the Supreme Court, the Attorney-General of

Minnesota recited a given series of statistics which detailed the dimensions of the economic slump in the state. For example, production of iron, the second most important industry after farming, was down to 15% of its normal level. Tax delinquencies were very high, rising to about 50% in parts of Minnesota. There could be little doubt that Minnesota was in the depth of a depression. 290 US 398, 423, 4.

6 Article 1, Section 10.

7 290 US 398, 475.

8 Although Sutherland wrote the dissent, initially it was assigned to Justice Van Devanter. In fact, Van Devanter had researched the historical circumstances surrounding the introduction of the contract clause and it was Van Devanter who had led the dissenting group of justices in conference. Unfortunately he had then fallen ill and Sutherland was thereupon assigned the task. But according to Van Devanter Sutherland 'wrote in his best style and did it nearly as perfectly as is possible. From beginning to end, citations, reasoning and all, the dissent follows my presentation in conference. When Justice Sutherland had finished the dissent he brought it over to me for criticism, saying that he had endeavoured to reproduce what I said.' Justice Van Devanter in a letter to his sister, Mrs John W. Lacy, dated 23 January 1934, Willis Van Devanter Papers, Box 16, Letter book 47, Manuscript Division, Library of Congress.

9 290 US 398, 475.

10 *Ibid.*, p. 428 (emphasis added).

11 *Ibid.*, p. 454 *passim*. For a different and rather tendentious historical interpretation of the contract clause see C. A. Miller, *The Supreme Court and the Uses of History* (1969), pp. 39–51.

12 1 How. 311 (1834).

13 *Ibid.*, p. 320 (emphasis added).

14 163 US 118 (1896).

15 24 How. 461 (1860).

16 See *McCracken* v. *Hayward*, 2 How. 608 (1844); *Gantly* v. *Ewing*, 3 How 707 (1845); *Walker* v. *Whitehead*, 16 Wall. 314 (1872).

17 256 US 170 (1921).

18 256 US 179 (1921).

19 258 US 242 (1922).

20 290 US 398, 440.

21 256 US 170, 198.

22 S. Hendel, *Charles Evans Hughes and the Supreme Court* (1951), p. 179.

23 290 US 398, 425.

24 *Ibid.*, pp. 439, 440 (emphasis added).

25 *Ibid.*, p. 445.

26 Charles Evans Hughes Papers, Box 157, Manuscript Division, Library of Congress.

27 Both Cardozo and Stone, in their different ways, suggested to Hughes that the economic conditions facing the nation at the time were unique in their severity. Stone declared that because of the depression, 'the whole economic structure of society is threatened'. Thus they both felt the Supreme Court should finally declare the Minnesota legislation constitutional, even if it meant that the decision was in Cardozo's words, 'inconsistent with things that they [the farmers] believed or took for granted [as they could] . . . not see changes in the relation between states and nation or in the play of social forces that lay hidden in the womb of time'. Harlan Fiske Stone Papers, Boxes 60, 75, Manuscript Division, Library of Congress.

28 Cardozo was satisfied with Hughes' final draft, which had incorporated several

of his suggestions. He scribbled on his proof sheet: 'I fully concur in this memorable opinion.' Hughes Papers, Box 157. Interestingly, Pusey incorrectly attributes Cardozo's remarks to Brandeis. See M. Pusey, *Charles Evans Hughes* (1952), Vol. 2, p. 698. Stone, however, at one and the same time contrived to be dissatisfied with the opinion and irritated by the praise Hughes subsequently received which he felt would have been more appropriately directed at himself. His secretary at the time of *Blaisdell*, Miss G. A. Jenkins, later wrote a brief note about Stone's memorandum and his version of the events surrounding the case: '. . . Stone was inclined, at first to write a concurring opinion, stronger than the majority opinion written by Hughes, C.J. He changed his mind and wrote the memorandum, taking it down personally to the Chief. The Chief's opinion then incorporated most of the points brought out by H.F.S. As it was rewritten incorporating H.F.S.'s views it was accepted by Brandeis and Cardozo who, with Stone, were formerly of the opinion that it was a poor opinion . . . The opinion was given such widespread publicity and C.E.H. praised so highly one article likening him to Marshall that I think H.F.S. was cured and will write his dissents and concurrences in the future, for all his hesitations to do so.' Stone Papers, Box 60. See also A. T. Mason, *Harlan F. Stone: Pillar of the Law* (1956), pp. 364–5.

29  290 US 398, 472.
30  *Op. cit.*, note 27.
31  Although Sutherland does not explicitly say that he thinks the Rent Cases went wrong, he certainly gives a strong impression that his feelings lie in that direction. 290 US 398, 478–9.
32  *Ibid.*, p. 442 (emphasis added).
33  *Ibid.*, p. 448.
34  *Ibid.*, p. 443.
35  Pusey, Vol. 2, pp. 699–700.
36  4 Wheat. 316 (1819). It is interesting to note that the Marshall quotation was borrowed from Cardozo's intended concurring opinion. In fact most of the dramatic and forceful language in the Chief Justice's opinion derived from either Cardozo's draft or Stone's memorandum. This is easily established because Hughes' response to Cardozo and Stone was to include a section in his opinion incorporating their suggestions. 'It is manifest . . . Minnesota mortgages to New York leases.' 290 US 398. A draft then of this passage was sent to Stone on 4 January 1934, who did not raise any further objections. Stone Papers, Box 60.
37  Holmes wrote, 'when we are dealing with words that are also a constituent act, like the Constitution of the United States, we must realise that they have called into life a being the development of which could not have been foreseen completely by the most gifted of its begetters. The case before us must be considered in the light of our whole experience and not merely in that of what was said a hundred years ago.' 252 US 416, 433 (1920).
38  Commenting on *Blaisdell*, the *New York Herald Tribune* said that 'great political significance was attached with the fact that Chief Justice Charles Evans Hughes joined the so-called liberal group of the court . . .', 9 January 1934, p. 1. The *New York Times* declared that 'for the present, the country will be disposed to say: *Roma dixit causa finita est.*' 10 January 1934, p. 20. Pusey claims that 'there was wide rejoicing throughout the country over the broad scope and realistic tone of the Chief Justice's opinion'. Pusey, Vol. 2, p. 700.
39  Indeed even in the area of contractual obligations concerning mortgages the Supreme Court post-*Blaisdell* held two Arkansas statutes which modified existing contracts to be unconstitutional. See *Worthen Co.* v. *Thomas*, 290 US 426 (1934), and *Worthen Co.* v. *Kavanagh*, 295 US 56 (1935).

**40** 291 US 502 (1934).

**41** Chapter 158, *Laws of New York*, 1933.

**42** 291 US 502, 511 (1934).

**43** *Ibid.*, pp. 518, 522.

**44** *Ibid.*, pp. 519, 520.

**45** *People* v. *Nebbia*, 262 NY 259 (1933).

**46** 291 US 502, 507.

**47** *Ibid.*, p. 505.

**48** Arthur E. Sutherland, Jr. who subsequently was appointed Bussey Professor of Law at Harvard University. He was assisted by Arthur E. Sutherland.

**49** 94 US 113 (1877).

**50** M. R. Benedict, *Farm Policies of the United States 1790–1950* (1953), p. 84.

**51** *Ibid.*, p. 84.

**52** See Solon J. Buck, *The Granger Movement* (1933).

**53** *License Cases*, 5 How. 504 (1847).

**54** 94 US 113, 125 (1877).

**55** *Ibid.*, p. 125.

**56** C. Fairman, 'The so-called granger cases', V *Stanford Law Review* 592 (1953).

**57** 94 US 113, 126 (1877).

**58** *Ibid.*, p. 126.

**59** *Ibid.*, p. 134.

**60** *Ibid.*, p. 132.

**61** *Ibid.*, p. 141.

**62** M. Pusey, *Charles Evans Hughes* (1952), Vol. 2, p. 700.

**63** C. P. Magrath, *Morrison R. Waite: The Triumph of Character* (1963), p. 185.

**64** C. Fairman, 'The so-called granger cases', *op. cit.* note 56, pp. 656–9.

**65** 262 US 522 (1923).

**66** 273 US 418 (1927).

**67** 277 US 350 (1928).

**68** See E. S. Corwin, *Liberty Against Government* (1948); B. F. Wright, *Growth of American Constitutional Law* (1942). See also books cited in Chapter 2, notes 24 and 25.

**69** 291 US 502, 531 (1934).

**70** *Ibid.*, p. 517.

**71** *Ibid.*, p. 530.

**72** *Ibid.*, p. 524.

**73** *Ibid.*, p. 524.

**74** *Ibid.*, p. 523 (emphasis added).

**75** *Ibid.*, p. 525.

**76** *Ibid.*, p. 539.

**77** For an instance where the Supreme Court was 'burying' a doctrine but doing so covertly, see the legislative appointment cases particularly the change between *Colegrove* v. *Green*, 328 US 549 (1944), and *Baker* v. *Carr*, 309 US 186 (1962). For a commentary on this particular point see P. C. Neal, '*Baker* v. *Carr*: politics in search of law', in *Supreme Court Review* (1962); R. A. Maidment, 'Policy in search of law: the Warren Court from *Brown* to *Miranda*', 9 *Journal of American Studies* 301, (1975).

**78** 291 US 502, 536 (1934).

**79** *Ibid.*, p. 555 (emphasis added).

**80** *Ibid.*, p. 559.

**81** *Ibid.*, p. 539.

**82** *Ibid.*, p. 525.

**83** Quoted in A. T. Mason, *Harlan Fiske Stone: Pillar of the Law* (1968), p. 368.

# 4

## The New Deal in Court I: 'Hot Oil' to *Railroad Retirement Board et al.* v. *Alton Railroad Co. et al.*

I

On 15 June 1933 the Seventy-Third Congress adjourned. Senators and Representatives congratulated themselves on a most impressive legislative achievement. Fifteen major bills were enacted into law and regardless of their quality it was a testament to both congressional energy and presidential leadership.[1] The events of those 'Hundred Days' have been recounted many times and from very different perspectives, but most accounts agree that in the spring of 1933, Washington was alive with a sense of expectancy that had been absent from the capital for a long time. As Frederick Lewis Allen has written:

> The very air of Washington crackled. Suddenly this city had become unquestionably the economic as well as the political capital of the country, the focus of public attention. The press associates had to double their staffs to fill the demand for explanatory dispatches about the New Deal bills. And into Washington descended a multitude of men and women from all over the country.[2]

The New Dealers, themselves while fully aware of the seriousness of the nation's problems, were also exhilarated by the enormity of their task. It was an exciting time for them:

> The memories would not soon fade – the interminable meetings, the litter of cigarette stubs, the hasty sandwich at the desk . . . the ominous rumour passed on with relish, the call from the White House, the postponed dinner . . . the office lights burning into the night, the lilacs hanging in fragrance about Georgetown gardens while men rebuilt the nation over long drinks, the selflessness, the vanity, the achievement.[3]

In this atmosphere, they attempted to alleviate the effects of the depression with a plethora of suggestions for recovery and reform.

55

In those early days of the New Deal, both President Roosevelt and his advisers were preoccupied with recovery and were not concerned with what they saw as constitutional niceties. From the administration's perspective the nation's economic position was bleak and this, they believed, required a programme which experimented with policies as well as with administrative procedures. Thus in 1933 the Roosevelt administration was prepared to support policies that were based on doctrines and assumptions that, on the most favourable interpretation, rested in the constitutional equivalent of a twilight zone. But if the administration was blasé about constitutional proprieties in 1933, it was decidedly less so in 1934 and 1935. For as time passed the constitutionality of New Deal legislation was being increasingly challenged in the lower courts and the administration correspondingly grew more aware of the judiciary and its power.

The administration's increased awareness of the legal process inevitably focused on the United States Supreme Court. The view of the administration was little different from those opinions expressed at the time or subsequently.[4] According to Rexford Tugwell: 'At the far right were the four hard Tories: Willis J. Van Devanter, Pierce Butler, James Clark McReynolds and George Sutherland. At the far left were the three Liberals: Harlan Fiske Stone, Louis Dembitz Brandeis and Benjamin N. Cardozo. In the center were Owen J. Roberts and above all, the Chief Justice, Charles Evans Hughes.'[5] This avowedly political conception of the Supreme Court would normally have held little comfort for the Roosevelt administration. After all on Tugwell's own analysis there were more 'Tories' than 'Liberals' and furthermore the 'swingmen' were viewed with the gravest suspicion. Roberts was an ex-corporation-lawyer who could not be trusted, and as for the Chief Justice, he was, as Felix Frankfurter wrote in 1937, 'as political as the President'[6] but with presumably very different political interests. Paradoxically in 1935 this mode of analysis did contain come crumbs of comfort for the administration. The Supreme Court's judgements in *Blaisdell* and *Nebbia* had led some observers to believe that 'swingmen' and the 'Liberals' had joined in a united front to provide the administration with a clean bill of constitutional health. 'For the time being it appeared that the constitutional crises brewing . . . might be averted. The Blaisdell and Nebbia decisions were widely read as showing the Supreme Court's stand on crucial New Deal legislation, gave Liberals fresh hope.'[7] Of course the united front did not transpire, which should have led to a questioning of the view that a court was just another political forum. But politicians, political commentators and political scientists who, as it were, had 'domesticated' judicial institutions were very reluctant to abandon this perception even when 'conservatives' voted for the TVA and 'liberals' against the NRA[8] And so the idea of judge as politician continued to dominate the imagination and to provide the reference for most analyses of the judicial response to the New Deal.

The New Deal came to the Supreme Court gradually. The first case involving a New Deal statute was not decided before 7 January 1935, but in the succeeding sixteen months the Court ruled on several major pieces of legislation.[9] This chapter does not claim nor will it attempt to provide a comprehensive account of all the cases that came before the Court in those sixteen months; the principal area of interest is economic regulation and in that context the most significant cases were *Schechter Brothers Poultry Corporation* v. *United States*,[10] *United States* v. *Butler*[11] and *Carter* v. *Carter Coal Co.*[12] However, other cases will be considered in order to provide a more extensive basis for an evaluation of the substance and style of judicial decision-making of the Hughes Court between 1934 and 1936. Some of these cases will not necessarily be centrally concerned with economic regulation but nevertheless should illustrate the processes of decision-making used by the Court. As with *Blaisdell* and *Nebbia*, it will be argued that opinions, both majority and minority, were constructed as a framework of constitutional intent, history and legal rules within which the established processes of argument and reasoning of the common law tradition were applied. In that sense *Blaisdell* and *Nebbia* were indicators of the future. They were not harbingers of a new liberal constitutionalism but a manifestation of a mode of judicial decision-making which was also to be applied to the New Deal statutes.

## II

The first New Deal statute to come before the Supreme Court was the National Industrial Recovery Act.[13] In the 'Hot Oil' case, as it was commonly known, only one section of that Act, 9(c), was being constitutionally questioned, as well as an order issued under the authority of that section. Section 9(c) of Title I of the National Industrial Recovery Act regulated certain aspects of the petroleum industry. The petroleum industry, like many others during the depression, suffered from overproduction, and the Roosevelt administration's remedy was to lower output through the establishment of production quotas which were to be administered by the state governments. Section 9(c), in particular, authorised the President, 'to prohibit the transportation in interstate and foreign commerce of petroleum and the products thereof produced or withdrawn from storage in excess of the amount permitted to be produced or withdrawn from by any . . . duly authorized agency of a State.'[14] Under this authority President Roosevelt had issued an executive order on 19 August 1933, approving a 'Code of Fair Competition for the Petroleum Industry' One of the provisions of this Code, Article III, Section 4 declared that, 'any production by any person . . . in excess of any such quota assigned to him, shall be deemed an unfair trade practice and in violation of this code.'[15] Under Title I of the National Industrial Recovery Act all such violations of a Code were punishable by a fine of 'not more than $500 for each offence, each day of said violation to be deemed a separate offence'.[16] Two Texas oil companies, the Panama Refining Company and the Amazon Petroleum Corporation, sued to restrain the responsible state officials from enforcing the Code. The companies argued that the Petroleum Code was unconstitutional under the Fourth and Fifth Amendments to the Constitution. Furthermore they claimed that Section 9(c) was invalid for transgressing the limitations imposed by the commerce clause as well as for an unconstitutional delegation of legislative power.

On 7 January 1935 the Supreme Court announced its decision. The Court was divided with Mr Justice Cardozo providing the solitary dissenting voice from Chief Justice Hughes' opinion. The majority opinion disposed of the arguments over the

Petroleum Code's constitutionality quickly. The Code of 19 August 1933 had been amended a few weeks later on 13 September. Due to an administrative oversight Article III, Section 4 had been omitted from the amended Code. However officials continued to operate on the assumption that the offending section was still effective, and so indeed did the plaintiffs. They had requested the Court to restrain the defendants from enforcing that particular section of the Petroleum Code. But as the Chief Justice pointed out: 'the attack in this respect was upon a provision which did not exist . . . When this suit was brought, or when it was heard, there was no cause of action for the injunction sought with respect to the provision of Section 4 of Article III of the Code; as to that, there was no real basis for controversy.'[17] The government had reinstated the section under a further amendment to the Code on 25 September 1934. Hughes responded to this by saying: 'If the Government undertakes to enforce the new provision, the petitioners . . . will have an opportunity to present their grievance . . . in the light of the facts as they will then appear. For this reason. . . we express no opinion as to the interpretations or validity of the provisions of the Petroleum Code.'[18]

Hughes then turned to the more substantial question of the constitutionality of Section 9(c). The plaintiffs had argued that 9(c) was invalid because it resulted from an unconstitutional delegation of legislative power and that it also overstepped the boundaries established by the commerce clause. Hughes took these propositions sequentially and examined the unconstitutional delegation contention first. If there had not been an improper delegation he would then evaluate the commerce clause proposition, but if there had been an unconstitutional delegation of legislative power, then there was no need for the Court to go any further. There was no need for the Court to go any further as Hughes did indeed find that Section 9(c) was based on an unconstitutional delegation of legislative power. How did the Chief Justice arrive at this assessment? The essential framework within which he conducted his evaluation of 9(c) is evident in the following passage:

> Assuming . . . the Congress has power to interdict the trans-
> portation of that excess in interstate . . . commerce, the question
> whether that transportation shall be prohibited by law is obviously

> one of legislative policy. Accordingly we look to the statute to see
> *whether Congress had declared a policy with respect to that subject;*
> *whether the Congress has set up a standard for the President's action;*
> *whether the Congress has required a finding by the President in the*
> *exercise of the authority to enact the prohibition.*[19]

Thus Hughes was arguing that control over 'hot oil' lay within the exercise of legislative power and if Congress wanted to delegate the execution of policy made under that power, then it would have to establish clear standards and guidelines for the President. For if there were no such standards, then the President would, in effect, be exercising the legislative power. What, in that case, was wrong with the President exercising the legislative power? The answer was that for the preceding two centuries, Americans had been conscious of the distinction between executive and legislative power.

At the time of the American Revolution a commonly-held belief among Americans was that the source of the problem between Britain and the colonies was that there had been a fusion of the executive and legislative power in government both in Britain and in the colonies.[20] Americans 'knew' from sources as diverse as John Locke[21] and Baron de Montesquieu[22] of the danger of such a fusion. In *Esprit des Lois*, Montesquieu had declared:

> When the legislative and executive powers are united in the same
> person, or in the same body of magistrates, there can be no liberty;
> because apprehensions may arise, lest the same monarch or senate
> should enact tyrannical laws to execute them in a tyrannical man-
> ner . . . There would be an end to everything, were the same man,
> or the same body . . . to exercise those . . . powers.[23]

Thus by 1776 there was a strong desire to put into effect what Maurice Vile has called a 'pure doctrine of the separation of powers' As Vile formulates it, the 'pure doctrine' requires for the

> establishment and maintenance of political liberty that the govern-
> ment be divided into three branches . . . the legislative, the
> executive and the judiciary. To each of these three branches there
> is a corresponding identifiable function of government, legislative,
> executive or judicial. Each branch of the government must be
> confined to the exercise of its own function and not allowed to

encroach upon the function of the other branches. Furthermore the persons who compose these three agencies. . . must be kept separate and distinct . . .'[24]

Several states such as Pennsylvania and Vermont adopted constitutions which were strongly influenced by the 'pure doctrine' although their experience was not entirely happy.[25] Thus by 1787 there was a movement away from the 'pure doctrine' to a position reflected in the American Constitution, of a modified separation: a position which granted the President a qualified veto power over legislation. Nevertheless Articles 1 and 2 of the Constitution stated the position clearly: 'All legislative powers herein granted shall be vested in a Congress of the United States . . . The executive power shall be vested in a President of the United States. . . .' Thus the Federal Convention not only made a distinction between the executive and legislative power but it also wanted the powers to be exercised by separate institutions.

When Hughes embarked on his evaluation of Section 9(c) of the National Industrial Recovery Act, he accepted as a matter of course that there was a legitimate and constitutionally proper role for delegation of power by the Congress:

> Undoubtedly legislation must often be adapted to complex conditions . . . with which the nation's legislature cannot deal directly. The constitution has never been regarded as denying to the Congress the necessary resources of flexibility and practicality . . . in laying down policies and establishing standards, while leaving to selected instrumentalities the making of subordinate rules within prescribed limits.[26]

Hughes accepted that there could be no flat fiat against delegation. Thus the argument returned to those questions mentioned earlier which were posited by the Chief Justice. Did Congress establish a policy on 'hot oil'? Did the Congress set a standard which would guide presidential action? Did the Congress require any finding by the President before he acted under the authority of 9(c)? The answer to each of those questions, claimed the Chief Justice, was no.

> In every case in which the question has been raised, the Court has recognised that there are limits of delegation . . . We think that

61

Section 9(c) goes beyond those limits . . . the Congress had declared no policy, has established no standard, has laid down no rule. There is no requirement, no definition of circumstances and conditions in which the transportation is to be allowed or prohibited.[27]

Thus Section 9(c) was unconstitutional.

The significance of the 'Hot Oil' case is not the factual finding that Section 9(c) of the National Industrial Recovery Act rested on an unconstitutional delegation of legislative power, but the reference within which the examination of such a proposition was conducted. The reference was constructed on the following principles: the legislative and executive powers were distinct but that did not imply that there could be no delegation by the Congress. Delegation was constitutional as long as Congress established a policy and standards by which the President could administer the legislation. The constitutional basis for such a reference was rooted in an American historical and constitutional experience. Interestingly Cardozo, who disagreed with Hughes' conclusion, did not dissent from the reference of the argument. Indeed he made it clear the disagreement between him and the majority was slight. 'My point of difference with the majority of the court is narrow.'[28] He too agreed that Congress could not delegate in a manner equivalent to issuing a blank cheque because that would be tantamount to handing over the legislative power to another body. 'I concede that to uphold the delegation there is need to discover in the terms of an act a standard reasonably clear whereby discretion must be governed.'[29] The disagreement between Cardozo and the rest was one of fact, not of constitutional interpretation, mode of reasoning or political attitude. Robert Jackson declared that the 'decision created a new obstacle to effective democratic government. It added a further perplexity in framing legislation.'[30] But his real complaint was that it 'was the first time a federal statute had been set aside on this ground'.[31] Jackson's implication was that the Court had created a makeshift legal principle to invalidate the Act. He was right inasmuch as it was the first time a federal law had been declared unconstitutional on these grounds but it was also the first time a federal statute had involved such a sweeping delegation of legislative power. Even

Justice Cardozo who felt that the delegation was proper resorted in an attempt to portray his understanding to a metaphor which one does not identify with precision. 'Discretion [in Section 9(c)] is not unconfined and vagrant. It is canalized within banks that keep it from overflowing.'[32] The problem was not as Jackson implied, with the Court, but with the National Industrial Recovery Act.


### III

When Roosevelt took office on 4 March 1933, he was not only faced with a domestic depression of unprecedented dimensions, he was also confronted with an international economic order in considerable disarray. Until the financial crisis had struck the major trading nations of the world, most governments had tied their currency to a gold standard which, if at the possible cost of economic expansion, had provided the international monetary system with stability. However in September 1931 the United Kingdom left the gold standard as did several other countries. Furthermore, restrictions were placed by these countries on the export of gold. By March 1933 only three countries – Holland, Switzerland and the United States – had not devalued their currency in terms of gold, which put them at some disadvantage in terms of international trade. The Roosevelt administration adopted a course of action designed to bring the United States into line with the remainder of the world, and so on 9 March 1933, the Emergency Banking Act was passed which authorised the President to halt the export and hoarding of gold. On 19 April the United States came off the gold standard and on 12 May 1933 President Roosevelt devalued the dollar by 40·94 per cent. The ramifications of these policies were many and varied, but one particular problem that had arisen as a consequence of this movement away from gold exercised the administration. The administration was concerned about the gold clauses that existed in both private and public contracts in the United States.

It was standard practice at the time for lawyers to insert a gold clause into private contracts. The purpose of it was straightforward; it was a device to ensure that the value of the debt was maintained in real terms. So gold clauses required that the repayment of the principal and the payment of interest would be payable 'in gold coin of the present standard of weight and fineness or . . . the equivalent in current money'.[33] Similarly the United States government issued bonds which contained a clause guaranteeing that 'the principal and interest hereof are payable in United States gold coin of the present standard of value'.[34] As long as the dollar continued in a stable and unchanging relationship with gold, these gold clauses remained dormant. However, after the devaluation of 12 May, the existence of these gold clauses meant that the dollar debt had been consequently increased by some 60 per cent. In 1934, the Attorney-General of the United States, Homer Cummings, estimated there was 100 billion dollars of contracted debt outstanding in the public and private sectors, but that if the gold clause in these various contracts were put into effect the level of overall indebtedness would increase by a further 69 billion dollars.[35] To prevent this occurrence the Congress on 12 June 1933 issued a Joint Resolution abrogating the effect of the gold clause in both private and public contracts.[36] The constitutionality of this Resolution was questioned in three cases that came before the Supreme Court which were decided on 10 January 1935.

The Three cases, *Norman* v. *Baltimore and Ohio Railroad Co.*,[37] *Nortz* v. *United States*[38] and *Perry* v. *United States*[39] raised very different issues. In the first case the authority of Congress to abrogate the gold clause in private contracts was challenged. In *Perry* the right of Congress to renege on its own gold clause guarantee was questioned. In both these cases the Court responded to the substantive claim. However, the claim in *Nortz* was disposed of on a narrow technical ground and is not germane to the discussion here.[40] The opinion of the Court, in all three cases, was written once again by Chief Justice Hughes and sustained by a majority of five to four. There was, however, a greater measure of agreement than the bare figures suggest. In *Baltimore and Ohio Railroad Co.* Hughes sustained the congressional authority to abrogate the gold clause in private contracts and there were four dissentients from his opinion, Justices Butler, McReynolds, Sutherland and Van Devanter. But in *Perry*, eight members of the Court, with the exception of Mr Justice Stone, shared Hughes' view that the Congress had no constitutional authority to vitiate the gold clause in government bonds. However, only four other judges, Justices Brandeis, Cardozo, Roberts and Stone, agreed with the Chief Justice's conclusion that as Perry had not suffered '. . . a loss. He is not entitled to be enriched.'[41] Thus the issues must be distinguished clearly in order to explain the various shades of opinion in these cases.

In *Norman* v. *Baltimore and Ohio Railroad Co.* Hughes conducted his examination of congressional authority to void the gold clause in private contracts within the following reference. The purpose of the Joint Resolution was to vitiate the gold clause in private contracts. This violation of contract *per se* did not put the Joint Resolution in constitutional jeopardy. The courts had always recognised the authority of Congress to affect private contractual obligations as long as the regulation was within the power of Congress. 'Contracts . . . cannot fetter the constitutional authority of the Congress. Contracts may create rights of property, but when contracts deal with a subject matter which lies within the control of the Congress, they have a congenital infirmity. Parties cannot remove their transactions from the reach of dominant constitutional power by making contracts about them.'[42] Thus the key question in this litigation was under what article of legislative power had the Congress issued the Joint Resolution? The Congress had done so under its power to establish a monetary system or, more specifically, under the authority granted to it under Article 1, Section 8 of the Constitution which granted Congress the power to 'coin money, regulate the value thereof and of foreign coin'. But of course this needed definition and did indeed receive judicial scrutiny in a series of cases arising out of government financial procedures during the Civil War.

Perhaps the most pressing problem facing the Lincoln administration, bar the dissolution of the Union, was the state of the Treasury. The problem, to put it simply, was appalling. There was an enormous shortfall between revenue and expenditure and there was no likelihood of the discrepancy being funded through taxation. Therefore the administration through the offices of its Secretary of the Treasury, Salmon Chase, urged the Congress to solve the financial embarrassment through a quite revolutionary suggestion. Ironically Chase was subsequently appointed to the

Supreme Court as Chief Justice and was on the bench when the constitutionality of his suggestion was decided. Chase's suggested solution to the Congress was that they grant government notes the quality of legal tender. Until 1862, the Congress had authorised only the production and issue of gold and silver coins; these coins and only these coins constituted legal tender in the United States. However, due to the financial stringency and despite misgivings, the Congress took Chase's advice, who it must be noted had his own qualms about the scheme. In February 1862, the first of the Legal Tender Acts were passed and 150 million dollars' of treasury notes were issued and they were to be 'legal tender in payment of all debts public and private in the United States'. In July 1862 and March 1863, two further issues of similar amounts were authorised by the Congress.[43] It was some seven years later that the US Supreme Court ruled on the constitutionality of these Acts in *Hepburn* v. *Griswold*[44] only to overrule itself some fifteen months later in the *Legal Tender Cases*.[45]

The history of the episode between *Hepburn* and the *Legal Tender Cases* does suggest that it was at the very least a curious episode in the Court's history. Firstly Justice Grier resigned. He was a member of the *Hepburn* majority although it is not entirely clear whether he fully understood the issues involved in the case. He resigned because he was infirm and because in 1869 Congress passed an act providing a salary for judges on resignation. In the same act a ninth seat was created on the Court and so there were two vacancies. Secondly, President Grant's nominee for Grier's replacement died and his nominee for the newly created seat was rejected by the Senate. Grant subsequently nominated Joseph Bradley and William Strong who were approved by the Senate. It was Bradley and Strong who joined with Justices Miller, Swayne and David in overruling *Hepburn*. This brief account does not do justice to the episode but the politics of the nomination process in 1869 is not entirely germane to the discussion at hand. What is relevant is the sweep of the opinion of the Court by Mr. Justice Strong and the concurrent opinion of Mr Justice Bradley in the *Legal Tender Cases*.[46]

The issue that faced the courts in the years immediately after the Legal Tender Acts was whether debts contracted in specie, gold or silver, could be repaid in the new greenbacks. In *Hepburn*, Chief Justice Chase held that Congress had no power to permit the repayment of debts resulting from contracts predating the Legal Tender Acts in greenbacks. But in the *Legal Tender Cases*, Strong and Bradley took a different view. Bradley's concurring opinion in particular took a very broad view of the powers of government over this matter.

> The United States is not only a government but it is a National Government, and the only government in this country that has the power of nationality. . . .Such being the character of the General Government, it seems to be a self-evident proposition that it is invested with all those inherent and implied powers which, at the time of adopting the Constitution were generally considered to belong to every government . . . This being conceded, the incidental power of giving such bills the quality of legal tender follows almost as a matter of course.[47]

Having thus disposed of the question of congressional authority to give these notes the quality of legal tender, Bradley turned to the issue of whether Congress could require creditors to accept greenbacks as payment. He confronted the issue in the broadest possible terms:

> There are times when the exigencies of the state rightly absorb all subordinate considerations of private interest, convenience or feeling; and at such times, the temporary though compulsory acceptance by a private creditor of the governmental credit in lieu of his debtor's obligation to pay, is one of the slightest forms in which the necessary burdens of society can be sustained. Instead of being a violation of such obligation, it merely subjects it to one of these conditions under which it is held.[48]

Thus the Legal Tender Acts were held constitutional and the Court's majority appeared to define the Constitution in a manner that granted the federal government a substantial discretion in its control over the monetary system. Inevitably Chief Justice Hughes relied on the opinion in these cases and was able to draw on their authority. In the *Legal Tender Cases*, the Supreme Court had ruled that Congress had the authority to select the precise manifestation of legal tender. The Congress could, if it so preferred, issue legal tender both in specie and in paper, and creditors could not indicate a preference for one form of legal tender over another, or rather they could indicate a preference but could not legally enforce the preference. The Congress, the Court decided in the *Legal Tender Cases*, had the authority to establish a uniform currency which could not be subverted by individual preference. Thus Hughes was able to argue in *Norman* v. *Baltimore and Ohio Railroad Co.* that in 1933 under the Joint Resolution the Congress had similarly acted to maintain a uniform currency. If the Congress had not, there would have been two types of currency, a dollar devalued by 40·94 per cent and a gold clause dollar. Therefore Hughes argued the Congress had the authority to remedy the position:

> We are concerned with the constitutional power of the Congress over the monetary system of the country . . . Exercising that power, the Congress has undertaken to establish a uniform currency, and parity between kinds of currency, and to make that currency, dollar for dollar, legal tender for the payment of debts. In the light of abundant experience, the Congress was entitled to choose such a uniform monetary system and to reject a dual system . . . within the range of the exercise of its constitutional authority.[49]

If the authority of the *Legal Tender Cases* was apparent to the majority in *Norman* v. *Baltimore Railroad Co.*, why was it not equally apparent to Mr Justice McReynolds? The *Legal Tender Cases* appeared to provide an impeccable judicial solution to the constitutional questions raised by the Joint Resolution. So why did Justices Butler, Sutherland and Van Devanter join in McReynolds' dissent? The answer lies with a case decided a week after the *Legal Tender Cases*. In *Trebilcock* v. *Wilson*[50] which was a reaffirmation of *Bronson* v. *Rodes*[51] a divided Supreme Court had ruled that where a contract specifically stipulated payment in specie, paper currency would not provide a satisfactory alternative. But this was partly taking away what the Court had granted to the Congress seven days earlier. In the *Legal Tender Cases* the Court had ruled that the Congress could impose a uniform currency, and that uniformity could not be challenged by individual preference. Furthermore the Congress's decision could override existing private contracts. But now in *Trebilcock* the Court appeared to be adding a rider to the proposition: if a contract specifically provided for payment in specie, it stood, regardless of congressional action. Mr Justice Bradley, who dissented, immediately saw the potential consequences in *Trebilcock*: 'Such a decision would completely nullify the power claimed for the government, for it would be very easy by the use of one or two additional words, to make all contracts payable in specie.'[52] Bradley's point was persuasive. The insertion of a few words in a private contract could in effect thwart the power granted to the Congress in the *Legal Tender Cases*. As a consequence of *Trebilcock*, presumably any congressional decision to ensure the equality of all forms of currency would be prevented by private contracts insisting on payment in one particular form, thereby creating a hierarchy of currency. The Supreme Court in *Trebilcock* and the *Legal Tender Cases* was facing in two, and indeed almost opposite, directions. Interestingly the Court in subsequent years sustained both the *Legal Tender Cases* in *Juillard* v. *Greenman*,[53] and the approach of *Trebilcock* v. *Wilson* in *Gregory* v. *Morris*.[54] But in *Norman* v. *Baltimore and Ohio Railroad Co.*, the Court was required to choose between the two alternatives.

The choice was made with the majority adopting the line of reasoning taken in the *Legal Tender Cases*. Why did they do so? Undoubtedly the Chief Justice was not blind to the financial repercussions which would flow from the invalidation of the Joint Resolution, just as Mr Justice Strong was aware of the financial effect if the Legal Tender Acts had been declared unconstitutional. Also, and more importantly, the Chief Justice with Brandeis, Cardozo, Roberts and Stone was clearly aware of the adaptive capabilities of the legal process. In *Blaisdell*, Hughes had shown he was conscious of the fact that judicial interpretation could be creative and that the process of common law reasoning allowed, indeed required, movement. Legal rules could not be static but demanded development. But, of course, judicial creativity should not be unbridled and the development that took place had to be conducted within a precise and delineated reference. The interesting characteristic about Hughes' opinion in *Norman* v. *Baltimore and Ohio Railroad Co.* is that the development that occurred was, in a sense, a move backwards. He merely restored the authority of the rule enunciated in the *Legal Tender Cases* and overruled the limitations suggested by *Trebilcock* and its successors. Thus *Norman* v. *Baltimore and Ohio Railroad Co.* was not a great step forward or even an illustration of creative judicial writing such as *Blaisdell*; it was, in essence, a clarification of a confused position. The fact that McReynolds and the rest of the minority did not agree with the Chief Justice's opinion is not evidence of politics as is frequently suggested. McReynolds' opinion does not violate any canons of judicial propriety. He did not invent a limitation of Congressional control over the monetary system. He did not propose any new arguments or stake out a new outpost from which the courts could launch an attack on the powers of the political branches. Instead McReynolds followed a line of authority articulated by earlier courts. The fact that he chose *Trebilcock* rather than the *Legal Tender Cases* is evidence not of political bias, but perhaps of a less fluid conception of the legal process. However, the point that cannot be emphasised too strongly is that the opinions of Hughes and McReynolds are not a world apart as some would suggest.[55] Instead Hughes and McReynolds shared a common framework and an identical reference within which the issues in the case were discussed. They adopted the same style of reasoning and argument. Admittedly, they did arrive at differing conclusions, but that is almost a minor point of dissension compared with the broad expanse of shared agreement. This similarity of outlook could, in subsequent cases, as it had in the past, also unite the Court. A degree of unity was evident in *Perry* v. *United States*.

In this case, the Supreme Court was asked to review congressional authority over contractual obligations entered into by the United States government. The plaintiff in this case, John Perry, had purchased a Liberty Bond issued by the government on 28 September 1918. The Bond contained the following clause: 'The principal and interest hereof are payable in United States gold coin of the present standard of value.'[56] It was, as Hughes pointed out, quite clear what the clause was intended to convey to a potential purchaser of government bonds: 'We think that the reasonable import of the promise is that it was intended to assure one who lent his money to the Government and took its bond that he would not suffer loss through the depreciation of currency.'[57] Thus when the Congress passed the Joint Resolution it was not only vitiating gold clauses in all contracts, it was also reneging on the government's own obligations. In *Norman* v. *Baltimore and Ohio*

*Railroad Co.*, Hughes concluded that there was congressional authority to nullify the gold clause in private contracts. But in *Perry* the Court's response was very different. The Chief Justice established quickly and easily, relying in particular on the *Sinking-Fund Cases*,[58] that authority lay with the view that Congress could not modify its own binding obligations. Firstly he distinguished the issues in *Perry* from those in *Norman*: 'There is a clear distinction between the power of Congress to control or interdict the contracts of private parties . . . and the power of the Congress to alter or repudiate the substance of its own engagements when it has borrowed money under the authority which the Constitution confers.'[59] Hughes then turned to the central point in the litigation:

> The Constitution gives to the Congress the power to borrow money on the credit of the United States, an unqualified power . . . The binding quality of the promise of the United States is of the essence of the credit which is so pledged. Having this power to authorize the issue of definite obligations for the payment of money borrowed, the Congress had not been vested with authority to alter, or destroy those obligations . . . This Court has given no sanction to such a conception of the obligations of our Government.[60]

No-one dissented from Hughes' conclusion. Admittedly the Court was divided over Perry's entitlement to relief, but on the substantive issue of constitutional interpretation there was no disagreement.[61] There was no disagreement because the divisions between so-called 'liberals', 'swingmen' and 'conservatives' have been exaggerated.

### IV

The next New Deal law to come before the Supreme Court was the Railroad Retirement Act of 1934.[62] This Act, strictly speaking, was not a New Deal measure as it had not been originally proposed by the Roosevelt administration. However, after the bill had passed the Congress, the President had signed it with enthusiasm because it was 'in line with the social policy of the Administration'.[63] The Retirement Act had been passed by the

Congress, in the words of the Assistant Attorney General of the United States, Harold Stephens, 'to promote economy and improve employee morale and promote the efficiency and safety of interstate transportation'.[64] The Congress believed that legislation was necessary because morale was low in the railroad industry as a consequence of financial insecurity. The voluntary pension programmes of the railroad companies did not alleviate the anxiety as they were inadequate. The company schemes did not provide, according to the Congress, their employees with a sense of security. Therefore the Congress passed the Railroad Retirement Act which imposed a compulsory pension scheme on the entire industry. The Act created a fund into which contributions from employers and employees were paid. This fund was to be administered by a Retirement Board who were required to aware pensions to, '(1) employees of any carrier on the date of the passage of the Act; (2) those who subsequently become employees of any carrier; (3) those who within one year prior to the date of enactment were in the service of any carrier . . .'.[65] The Retirement Act's constitutionality was challenged by 137 railroad companies on the grounds that it violated the due process clause of the Fifth Amendment and that it breached the restrictions imposed by the Commerce Clause. The companies sought an injunction against the Act's enforcement which was awarded. The Retirement Board appealed against the injunction and also applied for a writ of certiorari from the Supreme Court which was awarded.

On 5 May 1935 the Supreme Court handed down its judgement in *Railroad Retirement Board et al.* v. *Alton Railroad Co. et al.* The Court, by the narrowest of majorities, declared that the Retirement Act was unconstitutional because, firstly, it did violate the due process clause of the Fifth Amendment. Secondly and irredeemably, the Court argued the Act was a regulation of interstate commerce which did not fall within the meaning of the Constitution. (The Commerce Clause claim in this case will not be discussed in any detail as judicial decision-making in the area of interstate commerce is dealt with in the *Schechter* case and in *Carter* v. *Carter Coal*.)[66]

The opinion of the Court was written by Mr Justice Roberts and notably in this case he found himself on the opposite side to the

Chief Justice, who was the author of the minority opinion. Interestingly the disagreement between Roberts and Hughes in *Retirement Board* and subsequently *Carter* v. *Carter Coal* did not bring about a re-evaluation of the 'swingmen' allegation. Rather it has led to what may be seen as a refinement of the idea. Fred Rodell has suggested that the absence of the Chief Justice from the majority can be explained by the fact that Roberts plus Butler, McReynolds, Van Devanter and Sutherland were, at earlier stages in their respective careers, railroad lawyers.[67] Irving Brant discerned a Machiavellian characteristic in the Chief Justice's behaviour: 'When Charles Evans Hughes is a liberal he proclaims it to the world. When he is a reactionary, he votes silently and allows somebody else to be torn to pieces by the liberal dissenters.'[68] If Arthur Schlesinger Jr is to be believed, the Chief Justice changed his position on tactical grounds and cast his vote in a manner which would maintain his control over his colleagues. But did not constitutional issues and legal argument affect Hughes? According to Schlesinger, they did not affect Hughes' strategy: 'The course created no particular technical problem. A judge of Hughes' skill could make the close constitutional cases come out one way or the other with equal ease.'[69] Schlesinger's conception of constitutional interpretation is entirely instrumental. It is a weapon or device to be used in the attainment of a non-legal objective. Hughes and Roberts presumably disagreed in *Retirement Board* because their objectives, whatever they were, temporarily diverged. Their disagreement, according to this view, bore little relation to the material under discussion in the case. This style of analysis may be said to be misconceived. The disagreement between Hughes and Roberts in *Retirement Board* is interesting precisely because of their similarities in judicial style. They were cautious but flexible jurists. They were far more flexible than their historical reputation suggests. Both Hughes and Roberts had subtle minds which allowed them to see possibilities, which escaped some of their brethren, and to use these possibilities creatively and intelligently. Nevertheless, they were both fully aware of the limitations and requirements of the judicial function, which prevented too many overly creative excursions into the unknown. So why then did they disagree about *Retirement Board*? The answer mainly lies within the nature of adjudication over the vexed subjects of due process and interstate commerce. These have always been areas where judges were required to be subtle in order to achieve a delicate balance. Indeed, delicacy characterises the Court's decision-making in these two spheres, but whether the judiciary achieved a satisfactory balance is a more tendentious question. The brief account of due process and economic regulation in Chapter 2 above hopefully establishes that the Court was not divided over the general propositions that governed the reference within which the cases were argued and decided. Instead the judicial debate was over the exact location of the perimeter that ran between governmental authority and private property rights. Similarly over the Commerce Clause there was enormous difficulty in establishing with any precision the boundary between federal and state zones of authority.[70] It is thus hardly surprising that like-minded judges would, from time to time, disagree over these matters, and the issues in *Retirement Board* illustrate this point.

Roberts began his evaluation of the Railroad Retirement Act by examining the respondent's claim that it violated the due process protections of the Fifth Amendment. Superficially, at least, the companies appeared to have a point. For instance about 146,000 ex-employees, who had been in employment in the twelve months immediately before the Retirement Act became law, were eligible for a pension. But the Act did not distinguish between ex-employees, and consequently even those who had been discharged for a just cause were not entitled to a pension. Furthermore, their entitlement broke a principle of the Act that employer and employee should contribute to the fund. Thus the cost of the pensions for both ex-employees and those who were about to retire in years immediately after the passing of the Act had to be borne by the companies. Again, should any one of approximately one million ex-railroad workers be re-employed, even temporarily, then he would be entitled to a pension based on all his past service in the industry. But while these provisions of the Retirement Act were unhappy, they did not fatally damage it. Indeed Hughes agreed with Roberts' assessment that the provision concerning ex-employees was unconstitutional but nevertheless felt able to give the rest of the Act his imprimatur. The most serious due process problems arose from the Congress's decision to treat all the companies as a single employer. And it was on this provision that Roberts concentrated his heaviest fire: 'We conclude that the provisions of the Act which disregard the private and separate ownership of the several respondents, treat them all as a single employer, and post all their assets regardless of their individual obligations and the varying conditions found in their respective enterprises, cannot be justified as consistent with due process.'[71] How did Roberts justify his position?

Certain consequences flowed from the Congress's decision to treat all the railroad carriers as a single employer. The most important of the consequences was that there was a transference of resources between individual companies. Certain companies subsidised others as a result of the Act. There could be no doubt about that. On what basis were these transfers of wealth made? Certainly financial health was one of them. If in the very likely event that one corporation was unable to provide its contribution to the pension fund then the remaining companies would simply have to make up the shortfall. But financial well being was not the only basis on which these transfers took place. The age of employees for instance, was also a factor 'The probable age of entry into service of typical carriers differs materially; for one it is 28·4, for another 32·4, for a third 29·3 and for a fourth 34·2. Naturally the age of a person at date of employment will affect the resultant burden upon the contributors to the fund.'[72] Roberts then pointed to another consequence of the differing age composition of the workforces of the companies: 'The statute requires that all employees of age 70 must retire immediately. It is found that 56 of the respondents have no employees in that class. Nevertheless they must contribute toward the pensions of such employees of other respondents nearly $4,000,000 the first year and nearly $33,000,000 in total.'[73] Apart from the question of the transfer of resources between extant railroad corporations, there was the issue of the obligations imposed by the Act on the companies towards the employees of defunct corporations. Roberts observed that in recent years

> many carriers . . . have gone out of existence. The petitioners [The Retirement Board] admit that the employees of these defunct

carriers are treated upon exactly the same basis as the servants of existing carriers. In other words, past service for a carrier no longer existing is to be added to any service hereafter rendered to an operating carrier, in computing a pension the whole burden of payment of which falls on those carriers still functioning. And all the future employees of any railroad which discontinues operation must be paid their pensions by the surviving railroads.[74]

Thus the position, as Roberts saw it, was that the Congress's decision to treat the railroad companies as a single entity and pool their resources had certain consequences. Firstly, the Retirement Act reallocated the resources between the companies on a fairly arbitrary basis, i.e. the age composition of an individual corporation's workforce. Secondly, the Act imposed obligations on companies to the workforce of other railroads and to the former employees of defunct organisations: an obligation that was unexpected and unwelcome. In Roberts' judgement this was 'taking the property or money of one and transferring it to another without compensation . . .',[75] which was a violation of due process. But could the due process position be settled so easily? The answer was it could not and both Roberts and Hughes were aware of that.

In 1920 the Congress had passed the Transportation Act which dealt with the railroad corporations as a single entity and required 'the carriers to contribute one-half of their excess earnings to a revolving fund'.[76] In *Dayton-Goose Creek Railway Co.* v. *United States*,[77] the Supreme Court had sustained the constitutionality of the Act. Furthermore the Supreme Court had upheld the constitutionality of workmen's compensation laws which were based on the pooling-of-resources principle. In *Mountain Timber Co.* v. *Washington*,[78] a Washington state compensation law which obliged 'employers . . . to pay into a state fund certain premiums based upon the percentage of estimated payroll of the workmen employed'[79] in that industry, was upheld. On the strength of these two cases, Hughes felt able to declare that any objection to the Retirement Act based on due process was unfounded: 'The objection encounters previous decisions of the Court. We have sustained a unitary or group system . . . against the argument under the due process clause.'[80] Thus as Hughes perceived it the Retirement Act did not embody any new principle that the Court had not already validated. But Roberts' objection to the Act did not stem from a difference over principle. He did not object to the unitary system *per se* but to the particular consequences of the unitary system in the Retirement Act. Therefore he argued that *Dayton-Goose* and *Mountain Timber Co.* could be distinguished. In the first case Roberts claimed that the Transportation Act of 1920 was upheld because it contained a provision which guaranteed 'each carrier a reasonable return upon its property devoted to transportation'.[81] Roberts was emphatic that in the absence of that provision or in the event of noncompliance with it the Act would have been held unconstitutional. Similarly in *Mountain Timber Co.* Roberts declared that the Washington Statute 'recognised the difference in drain or burden . . . and sought to equate the burden with the risk', whereas the 'Railroad Retirement Act, on the contrary . . . treats all the carriers as a single employer, irrespective of their several conditions'.[82] Thus Roberts was not disputing Hughes' assertion that there was no new principle at stake in the Retirement Act. He did not deny the right of Congress to treat the railroad industry as a single entity or for government to oblige employers to pool their resources. Indeed, how could he, as these were issues that already had been settled? The core of the disagreement between the two sides on the Court was not then of general principle, but of particularistic fact. Hughes and Roberts did not disagree over the nature and character of governmental power but over its particular manifestation in the Retirement Act, and indeed of one narrow aspect of its manifestation. They did not disagree over the substantive reference of due process adjudication. They shared an identical approach to evaluation due process claims. Their dispute was therefore located at the margin. But why then does one judge step to one side of the margin, and another to the opposite side? There is no satisfactory answer, particularly when the two judges are as similar as Hughes and Roberts.

Perhaps an answer or a partial answer lies with the material under judicial review. The Court was continually having to draw the boundary between governmental authority and property rights and inevitably the boundary was not only uneven, it was constantly moving, if only marginally. *Railroad Retirement Board et al.* v. *Alton Railroad Co. et al.*, in that context, was just another point or marker in the Court's plotting of the boundary. No new due process principle was announced in the case nor was an established principle disavowed. It was, as far as any appellate litigation can be, a commonplace case. The boundary between governmental authority and property rights was not markedly affected. It was, in other words, an ordinary case in legal terms. The disagreement between Hughes and Roberts in terms of constitutional development was minor and inconsequential, and certainly was not capable of sustaining the elaborate theories of judicial behaviour mentioned earlier in this section. But perhaps therein lies the problem of *Railroad Retirement Board*; it was a run-of-the-mill case but it was overlaid with unwarranted political significance. Ever since the Court ruled on the constitutionality of the Retirement Act, Roberts' opinion has rarely been analysed for its intrinsic qualities. Instead it has been used or seen as a guide to judicial attitudes towards other pieces of New Deal legislation that were to come before the Court. Roberts' judgement was interpreted as a statement of a new constitutional/legal doctrine, which it was not. It shared the underlying principles and doctrines of Hughes' opinion. Nevertheless, *Railroad Retirement Board et al.* v. *Alton Railroad Co. et al.* has developed the historical reputation as being the first major judicial setback to the New Deal and as the case that established the direction of the Court in the years 1934–36.[83] Whether it was a setback to the Roosevelt administration is not germane to the discussion here. But Roberts did not establish a direction for the Court, indeed he could not do so. After all, judges decide cases, not directions.

**NOTES**

1 The fifteen major pieces of legislation were:
  (a) 9 March 1933 – Emergency Banking Act
  (b) 20 March 1933 – Economy Act
  (c) 31 March 1933 – Civilian Conservation Corp.
  (d) 19 April 1933 – Gold Standard – abandonment of
  (e) 12 May 1933 – Federal Emergency Relief Act
  (f) 12 May 1933 – Agricultural Adjustment Act
  (g) 12 May 1933 – Emergency Farm Mortgage Act
  (h) 18 May 1933 – Tennessee Valley Authority Act
  (i) 27 May 1933 – Truth-in-Securities Act
  (j) 5 June 1933 – The Joint Resolution of Congress with respect to the Gold Clauses

(k) 13 June 1933 – Home Owners' Loan Act
(l) 16 June 1933 – National Industrial Recovery Act
(m) 16 June 1933 – Glass-Steagall Banking Act
(n) 16 June 1933 – Farm Credit Act
(o) 16 June 1933 – Railroad Co-ordination Act

2 F. L. Allen, 'New Deal honeymoon' in M. Crane (ed.), *The Roosevelt Era* (1947), p. 19. See also F. L. Allen, *Since Yesterday* (1942), p. 31.
3 A. M. Schlesinger Jr, *The Coming of the New Deal* (1965), p. 19.
4 See Chapter 2, pp. 43–8.
5 R. G. Tugwell, *The Democratic Roosevelt* (1957), pp. 386–7.
6 M. Freedman, *Roosevelt and Frankfurter: Their Correspondence 1928–1945* (1967), p. 402.
7 A. T. Mason, *Harlan Fisk Stone: Pillar of the Law* (1968), p. 367.
8 See *Ashwander* v. *Tennessee Valley Authority*, 297 US 288 (1936), *Schechter Brothers' Poultry corporation* v. *United States*, 295 US 495 (1935).
9 The fate of seven major pieces of legislation were decided between 9 January 1935 and 18 May 1936. They were as follows:
   The Joint Resolution of Congress with respect to the Gold Clauses, 1933.
   The Railroad Retirement Act, 1934.
   The Frazier-Lemke Act, 1934.
   The National Industrial Recovery Act, 1933.
   The Agricultural Adjustment Act, 1934.
   The Tennessee Valley Authority Act, 1933.
   The Bituminous Coal Conservation Act, 1935.
10 295 US 495 (1935).
11 297 US 1 (1936).
12 298 US 238 (1936).
13 *Panama Refining Co. et al.* v. *Ryan et al.*; *Amazon Petroleum Corp. et al.* v. *Ryan et al*, 293 US 388 (1935).
14 *Ibid.*, p. 406.
15 *Ibid.*, p. 410.
16 *Ibid.*, p. 410.
17 *Ibid.*, pp. 412, 413.
18 *Ibid.*, p. 413.
19 *Ibid.*, p. 415 (emphasis added).
20 See M. J. C. Vile, *Constitutionalism and the Separation of Powers* (1967), pp. 126–32.
21 See P. Laslett (ed.), *John Locke: Two Treatises of Government* (1963), pp. 132–5, 401–13.
22 *Ibid.*, Baron de Montesquieu, *Esprit des Lois* (1900).
23 *Ibid.*, pp. 151, 152. See also M. Richter, *The Political Theory of Montesquieu* (1977), pp. 84–93.
24 Vile, *Constitutionalism*, *op.cit*, note 20, p. 13.
25 *Ibid.*, pp.140–154.
26 293 US 388, 421 (1936). See also *United States* v. *Grimaud*, 220 US 506 (1911).
27 293 US 388, 430 (1936).
28 *Ibid.*, p. 434.
29 *Ibid.*, p. 434.
30 R. Jackson, *The Struggle for Judicial Supremacy* (1941), p. 95.
31 *Ibid.*, p.94.
32 293 US 388, 440 (1935).
33 294 US 240, 279 (1935).
34 294 US 330, 347 (1935).

35  294 US 240, 256 (1935).
36  48 Stat. 113 (1933).
37  294 US 240 (1935).
38  294 US 317 (1935).
39  294 US 330 (1935).
40  *Nortz* was decided on whether the Court of Claims had authority over the action brought in this case, 294 US 317, 327 (1936).
41  294 US 330 (1935).
42  294 US 240, 307, 308 (1935). See also *Hudson Water Co.* v. *McCarter*, 209 US 349 (1908).
43  For a particularly distinctive analysis of the Greenback episode see, M. Freidman and A. J. Schwarz, *A Monetary History of the United States, 1976–1960* (1971), pp. 15–88.
44  8 Wall. 603 (1870).
45  12 Wall. 457 (1871).
46  For a detailed and interesting account of the nominations of Bradley and Strong see C. Fairman, *History of the Supreme Court of the United States: Reconstruction and Reunion 1864–88, Part One* (1971), pp. 677–776. See also Fairman's excellent biography of Mr Justice Miller, *Mr Justice Miller and the Supreme Court 1862–1890* (1939), pp. 149–78.
47  12 Wall. 457 (1871).
48  *Ibid.*, p.530.
49  294 US 240, 316 (1935).
50  12 Wall. 457 (1871).
51  7 Wall. 229 (1869).
52  12 Wall. 457 (1871).
53  110 US 421 (1884). See also *Ling Su Fan* v. *United States*, 218 US 302 (1910).
54  98 US 619 (1878).
55  See J. Paschal, *Mr. Justice Sutherland: A Man Against the State* (1951), pp. 179–82. Paschal like so many commentators on the period are anxious to emphasise McReynolds' occasional outbursts rather than the sober arguments in the opinion.
56  293 US 330, 347 (1935).
57  *Ibid.*, p. 349.
58  99 US 700 (1879).
59  294 US 330, 350, 351 (1935).
60  *Ibid.*, p. 351.
61  In his concurring opinion in *Perry*, Stone reasoned that as the plaintiff was not entitled to relief, the Court was not obliged to rule on the substantive issues raised in the case. However, there is little doubt as to how he would have cast his vote if he believed that the issue had to be resolved. 'The Government's refusal to make the stipulated payment . . . is . . . a repudiation of its undertaking . . . I deplore this refusal to fulfil the solemn promise of bonds of the United States'. 294 US 330, 359 (1935).
62  48 Stat. 1283 (1934).
63  R. Jackson, *The Struggle for Judicial Supremacy* (1941), p. 104.
64  295 US 330, 335 (1935).
65  *Ibid.*, p. 345.
66  *A.L.A. Schechter Poultry Corp. et al.* v. *United States*, 295 US 495 (1935), *Carter* v. *Carter Coal Co.*, 298 US 238 (1936).
67  F. Rodell, *Nine Men* (1955), pp. 30–1.
68  Irving Brant, 'How liberal is Justice Hughes?', *New Republic*, 21 July 1937, p. 28.
69  A. Schlesinger Jr, *The Politics of Upheaval* (1966), pp. 466, 467.

70 For an extended discussion of the Commerce Clause see E. Corwin, *The Commerce Power versus States Rights* (1936); F. Frankfurter, *The Commerce Clause under Marshall, Taney and Waite* (1937); B. Gavit, *The Commerce Clause of the United States Constitution* (1932).

71 295 US 330, 360 (1935).

72 *Ibid.*, p. 355.

73 *Ibid.*, p. 355.

74 *Ibid.*, p. 356.

75 *Ibid.*, p. 357.

76 *Ibid.*, p. 358.

77 263 US 456 (1923).

78 243 US 219 (1917).

79 295 US 330, 359 (1935).

80 *Ibid.*, p. 385.

81 *Ibid.*, p. 358.

82 *Ibid.*, p. 359, 360.

83 W. Murphy, *Congress and the Court* (1962), p. 55.

## 5

# The New Deal in Court II: 'Black Monday'

I

On 27 May 1935 the Supreme Court announced three unanimous decisions. Firstly, the Court ruled that the President's power to remove a commissioner of the Federal Trade Commission was limited to the specific causes for removal enumerated in the Federal Trade Commission Act of 1914. Consequently, the Court declared, President Roosevelt's removal of Commissioner William E. Humphrey had been invalid.[1] Secondly, the Court struck down the Frazier-Lemke Act which was an amendment to the federal Bankruptcy Act.[2] Finally and most noteworthy the Court held the National Industrial Recovery Act unconstitutional.[3] It was 'Black Monday'. Curiously the Court's decisions did not make a great deal of material difference. Undoubtedly the Roosevelt administration would miss the Frazier-Lemke Act as it was popular with farmers. But the decision in *Humphrey's Executor* v. *United States* could have little practical effect as Commissioner Humphrey had died. And so, in a sense, had the NRA.

> By the time the Supreme Court handed down its decisiong . . . the NRA had already lost most of its popularity and support. Not many congressmen were enthusiastic about the program, and the chances for renewal had become increasingly slim. Businessmen . . . hailed the Schechter decision. . . . And many New Dealers seemed glad to be rid of the . . . NRA. The whole thing Roosevelt confided to Frances Perkins had been an 'awful headache'.[4]

Nevertheless the administration felt obliged to respond and in a press conference President Roosevelt lamented the Court's adoption of a 'horse-and-buggy definition of interstate commerce'.[5] Privately he was furious. 'Well, where was Ben Cardozo? And what about old Isaiah?'[6] For even if there had been no substantive damage to the New Deal, 'Black Monday' had been a political embarrassment. It was an embarrassment because, if for no other reason, the administration could no longer place the blame for its judicial problems on the shoulders of the conservatives and 'swingmen'. Some two years later, President Roosevelt in his broadcast on the Judiciary Reorganisation Bill, complained about various judicial decisions but pointedly avoided any reference to the 'Black Monday' cases.[7] Clearly the administration was discomforted by 'Black Monday', but it should not have been surprised.

Two of the three 'Black Monday' cases involved New Deal measures that in one form or another constituted economic regulations and will be examined in some detail in this chapter. The first case, *A. L. A. Schechter Poultry Corp. et al.* v. *United States* concerned the National Recovery Administration (NRA), which had been, in the first fifteen months of the New Deal, the most exciting and vibrant agency of the federal government. Indeed in the first few months of its existence the NRA, to the general public, *was* the New Deal. Its administrator was Hugh Johnson who had the capacity to transform a 'government agency into a religious experience' and under his direction the nation was caught up in a bout of Blue Eagle fever.[8] But by 1935, as mentioned above, the NRA was in its death throes. Why had this happened? The answer principally lies with the way the NRA was created in 1933. It is a story that has been recounted several times but it is worth retelling briefly as it is relevant to the events in the *Schechter* case.[9]

When President Roosevelt took office on 2 March 1933, he and his advisers had no plans for major industrial reforms, but by 16 June of the same year the National Industrial Recovery Act was law. What had occurred in the intervening months? On 6 April the Senate had approved a thirty-hour-week bill sponsored by Senator Hugo Black and this had goaded the administration into doing something. Black's bill was not only inadequate and required replacement by a more suitable measure; it also convinced the administration of the need for more general legislative action on industrial matters. For the next two months there was feverish activity in the administration. A number of different groups were organised to develop ideas and draft bills. There was a group under Frances Perkins, the Secretary of Labor; there was another chaired by Raymond Moley, Assistant Secretary of State, and Hugh Johnson; and there was a further one organised by John Dickinson, Under-Secretary of Commerce, which had links with Senator Robert Wagner who was also contemplating an industrial reform measure. Inevitably these various groups provided different answers and indeed identified different problems and it is a minor achievement that by early May there were only two major drafts of an industrial reform bill, although there were striking differences between them. The President himself did not appear to mind which of the two drafts was finally adopted as long as there was agreement between all the participants. He suggested that they lock themselves in a room until they were in broad agreement. As Hugh Johnson recalled in his memoirs, 'we met in Lew Douglas's office. Lew, Senator Wagner, John Dickinson, Mr Richberg and myself with a few 'horners-in' from time to time'.[10] And they sat there until they had a mutually satisfactory draft. It was this draft that emerged as the National Industrial Recovery Act. The House of Representatives left the administration's proposal untouched and although the Senate did give the bill a rough passage, the Act was in essence the same as the administration's bill.

The National Industrial Recovery Act had three titles. Titles II and III dealt with public works and Title I with the nation's industrial structure. It was Title I that was the course of controversy, both political and legal. Under this Title, the President had the authority to approve codes of behaviour drawn up by trade or industrial groups, but in the event that there was no agreement within an industry over a code, the President was empowered to impose one. Congress offered the President, with one exception, only the most general guidance in the formulation of these codes. In Section 1, the Congress issued a declaration of principles which established certain general goals, such as the elimination of unfair practices and the reduction of unemployment, to guide the code makers, although in Section 7 which dealt with labour standards the Act did give more precise instructions as to how the codes should be formulated in this respect. These codes were exempt from anti-trust laws. Apart from the codes, Title I gave the President the power to license industries if he established that destructive wage-and-price cutting practices were taking place.

The Act also granted the President the authority to approve collective bargaining agreements between unions and business organisations and give these agreements legal effect. The President was additionally empowered to limit imports, and finally in Section 9, which has been dealt with above, he was given the power to regulate pipeline companies and prohibit the shipment of 'hot oil'.[11] In summary, Title I was a break with the past on two fronts. Firstly, it delegated an extraordinary grant of power to the executive branch. Secondly, it involved the federal government in an unprecedented manner in the nation's peace-time economy. Yet the National Industrial Recovery Act had not been formulated after a period of judicious consideration; there had been just three months between conception and birth. And those three months had been very hectic. The period was characterised by argument, confusion and above all compromise to achieve a temporary peace. Whether these conditions were suitable to frame legislation that affected the structure of American industry through hitherto untested procedures and regulations, is doubtful. As Ellis Hawley has written:

> Within the confines of a single measure . . . the formulators of the National Industrial Recovery Act had appealed to the hopes of a number of conflicting pressure groups. Included were the hopes of labor for mass organisation and collective bargaining, the hopes of businessmen for price and production controls, the hopes of competitive industries to imitate their more monopolistic brethren, the hopes of dying industries to save themselves from technological advance, and the hopes of small merchants to halt the inroads of mass distributors. Overlying these more selfish economic purposes [were] . . . conflicting ideologies . . . conflicting theories of economic recovery. For the time being the numerous conflicts had been glossed over by a resort to vagueness, ambiguity and procrastination. Congress . . . had simply written an enabling act . . . and . . . passed the buck to the Administration. The very nature of the act made . . . dissension . . . inevitable. In practice the NRA . . . was unable to define and enforce a consistent line of policy; and in this welter of conflict and confusion, it was scarcely surprising that the result turned out to be what Ernest Lindley called an 'administrative, economic and political mess'.[12]

It was the Supreme Court's task in *Schechter* to decide whether the

NRA was also a constitutional 'mess'

The decision to use *Schechter* as the test case for the constitutionality of the National Industrial Recovery Act was to a certain extent forced on the government. It had been assumed until 1 April 1935 that the fate of the Act would be decided in *United States* v. *Belcher* which involved the code promulgated for the lumber industry.[13] However, the Justice Department discovered an error in the government's brief which had been submitted before a lower court and consequently the Solicitor General, Stanley Reed, felt obliged to request a dismissal of the case, which was granted. This was a misfortune for the government for the facts in *Schechter* were particularly unfavourable to its cause. Robert Jackson noted: 'The case was far from ideal as a test case. The industry was not a major one, and the fair trade provisions ... were hardly calculated to electrify any Court to the need for federal regulation.'[14] Nevertheless the administration decided to press ahead as it was becoming increasingly concerned with a view that was gaining currency in the newspapers: 'There can be but one inference, from this extraordinary conduct, that the Justice Department felt sure that the NRA was in its fundamentals unconstitutional, and that the Supreme Court was about to hold so.'[15] In order to avoid any further charges of bad faith or cowardice, the administration decided to use the 'sick chicken' case as a test for the NRA. And so *A. L. A. Schechter Poultry Corp. et al.* v. *United States* was argued before the Supreme Court in early May 1935.

The case had arrived before the Supreme Court on a writ of certiorari. The Schechter Poultry Corp. had been found guilty of breaking the Live Poultry Code on eighteen separate counts.[16] However, the Circuit Court of Appeal had dismissed two of the convictions which were for violations of the Code that related to minimum wages and maximum hours of labour. The Court of Appeal had declared that these were areas of regulation which were not within the powers of the Congress, whereupon both the government and the Schechter Poultry Corp. appealed for a writ of certiorari. In their arguments before the Court, both sides realised the constitutionality of the Act would be decided within the legislative power. Consequently they addressed themselves to both these issues and so did the Court.

The opinion of the Court was written by Chief Justice Hughes and he took the issue of delegation first. Of course it had only been some seven months since the Court had spoken, once again through Hughes, on this very question in *Panama Refining Co. et al.* v. *Ryan et al.* So to what extent were the facts in *Schechter* different to those in *Panama Refining Co.*? The answer was, to an appreciable extent, but whether the government could take comfort from the difference was another matter. The facts in *Schechter* were that a Code had been approved in an executive order by President Roosevelt on 13 April 1934.[17] The Code had eight articles which were applicable to the live poultry industry in New York City and its environs. The eight articles governed amongst other things, the hours, wages, labour provisions and trade practices of the industry. The authority claimed by the President, when he approved the Code, was Section 3 of the National Industrial Recovery Act. But what guidelines did Section 3 offer the President when he exercised his discretionary approval? The answer would decide the statute's constitutionality at least in this respect.

The government's brief argued that the Congress provided two criteria which did indeed guide the President's exercise of his discretionary power of approval. Firstly, the codes created under Section 3 were to be codes of fair competition and the phrase did have a meaning. Secondly, in the event that fair competition did not by itself provide adequate guidance, then the statement of principles in Section 1 of Title I of the Act would embellish and add meaning to the words 'fair competition'. What then did fair competition mean? The government's brief did not provide a definition but it did suggest that 'fair competition' – has been used in the Federal Trade Commission Act'.[18] If fair competition was the antithesis of unfair methods of competition, what then did unfair methods of competition mean? There was no precise meaning to the phrase. When the Federal Trade Commission Act of 1914 was written, the expression 'unfair competition', which had a well-defined but limited common law meaning, was not used in preference to 'unfair methods of competition'. The Congress very deliberately refrained from providing a definition. The conference committee of both houses explained why it had abstained from doing so: 'It is impossible to frame definitions which embrace all unfair practices. There is no limit to human inventiveness in this field . . . If Congress were to adopt the method of definition, it would undertake an endless task.'[19] Instead the Congress left the task of interpreting the words to the Federal Trade Commission, a quasi-judicial body. The Commission investigated complaints of unfair methods of competition through a special and elaborate procedure established by the Congress. As the Chief Justice noted: 'Provision was made for formal complaint, for notice and hearing, for appropriate findings of fact supported by adequate evidence'.[20] At the culmination of this process, the Commission made a ruling which was open to judicial scrutiny. What it did not do was provide a definition or a meaning for unfair methods of competition. Thus fair competition in the NRA codes could not be defined in terms of unfair methods of competition. It could not be the antithesis of unfair methods of competition as the Federal Trade Commission and the courts were in the process of slowly and incrementally establishing the contours of that phrase. Fair competition by itself did not provide adequate guidance to the President. But was fair competition 'given further meaning and substance by . . . the policy set forth in Section 1 of the Act'?[21]

Section 1 of Title I of the National Industrial Recovery Act was placed under the heading 'Declaration of Policy' The first sentence of Section 1 declared an emergency; it then continued in the following manner:

> It is hereby declared to the policy of Congress to remove obstructions to the free flow of interstate and foreign commerce which tend to diminish the amount thereof; and to provide for the general welfare by promoting the organization of industry for the purpose of cooperative action among trade groups, to induce and maintain united action of labor and management under adequate governmental sanctions and supervision, to eliminate unfair competitive practices, to promote the fullest possible utilization of the present productive capacity of industries; to avoid undue restriction of production (except as may be temporarily required), to increase the consumption of industrial and agricultural products by increasing purchasing power, to reduce and relieve unemployment, to improve standards of labor, and otherwise to rehabilitate industry and to conserve natural resources.[22]

Was fair competition given further meaning and substance by Section 1? The answer in a sense was yes, but it was an elaborate answer. When the government brief had argued that fair competition was the antithesis of unfair methods of competition, the implication was that just as there were specific practices that were unfair, correspondingly there were specific practices that were fair. But the argument was disingenuous because the conception of a code of fair competition and the notion that lay behind the expression 'unfair methods of competition' were very different. Even if unfair methods of competition had not achieved a full and rounded definition, the suggestion that lay behind the phrase was evident. In 1914, the Congress clearly believed that there were particular business practices that were harmful and deleterious. This behaviour could manifest itself in various forms and so the Congress gave the Federal Trade Commission the task of identifying and stopping the proscribed activities. The task of the Commission was a negative one; it was to identify and stamp out particular abuses. But of course this left an absolutely enormous variety of business practices and procedures which were fair. Thus the difference between fair competition and unfair methods of competition can be seen. The idea behind unfair methods was that a limited number of practices should not be available to businessmen in the conduct of their affairs. These specific procedures should be proscribed from being legitimate options in business dealings, whereas fair competition codes implied that the entire spectrum of business activity should be regulated. It was a very different kind of proposition and indeed a much larger proposition. Fair competition codes were not merely the reverse side of the coin to unfair methods of competition, they were a new development in governmental regulation. It was debatable whether the Congress could impose such extensive regulations over industry, but even if Congress did have the authority, it could not delegate that authority without guidance. So did Section 1 give meaning to or impose limitations on the phrase 'codes of fair competition'?

Section 1 did give a meaning to fair competition. Congress declared, in that section, its objective which was the rehabilitation and recovery of American industry in particular and the economy in general. Thus a code of fair competition was that which furthered the objective of recovery and rehabilitation. It was a definition, but it was not of a more limited character than the earlier suggestion that fair competition was the antithesis of unfair methods of competition. Furthermore it did not provide any guidance to the President in the exercise of his discretionary power to approve or impose codes on individual industries. It was entirely a matter of presidential opinion whether a code of fair competition was helpful to recovery. There were no requirements, no rules, other than the guidelines suggested in Section 7 of Title I on labour provisions, which the President had to establish before he issued his approval. His approval was subject only to his judgement. It was within his gift to issue his imprimatur. As Mr Justice Cardozo, in his concurring opinion, wrote with more than a heavy hint of irony, 'here in effect is a roving commission to inquire into evils and upon discovery correct them'[23] In *Panama Refining Co.*, the court had reasserted the historically-established doctrine that legislative and executive powers were distinct, but the court accepted that legislative power could be delegated as long as Congress established a policy and standards which enabled a President to administer the legislation. In the National Industrial Recovery Act, the Congress had failed to provide such a policy and standards. The Chief Justice concluded:

> To summarize ... the Recovery Act is without precedent. It supplies no standards ... It does not undertake to prescribe rules of conduct ... Instead of prescribing rules of conduct, it authorizes the making of codes to prescribe them. For that legislative under-taking, section 3 sets up no standards aside from the statement of the general aims ... described in section 1. In view of the scope of that broad declaration ... the discretion of the President in approving or prescribing codes, and thus enacting laws for the government ... is virtually unfettered.[24]

Cardozo described the position more pithily. 'That is delegation running riot.'[25]

The Court then turned its attention to the claim that the Live Poultry Code and indeed the enabling legislation, Title I of the National Industrial Recovery Act, breached the limitations imposed by the Commerce Clause. The history of Commerce

Clause litigation, by 1935, was very substantial and so the words of Article 1, Section 8 that 'The Congress shall have power . . . To regulate Commerce with foreign Nations, and among the several States, and with the Indian Tribes' did not provide a great deal of assistance to the Court in *Schechter*. The existence of the Clause, however, was a reminder that the Articles of Confederation had not been a success partly because of a lack of national power to regulate commerce. Since 1787, and particularly since *Gibbons* v. *Ogden*[26] in 1824, the courts had shown that they were aware of the historical reasons for the Commerce Clause and of its importance. 'You would scarcely imagine', wrote Justice Miller, 'and I am sure you do not know, unless you have given some consideration to the subject, how very important is that little sentence in the Constitution.' It was 'one of the most prolific sources of national power'.[27] But appropriately and characteristically, the courts assumed that any grant of power, in an American constitutional context, was not unlimited. Consequently, the Congress's control over interstate commerce had always been deemed to be extensive but not unlimited. Of course, as with due process adjudication, both the location of the boundary which marked the extent of congressional power and the process by which the boundary was located became very contentious constitutional issues. But there was no way of avoiding the controversy.

The first important Commerce Clause case established the reference which courts have essentially used ever since. In *Gibbons* v. *Ogden*, the state of New York had granted to Ogden a monopoly over steamboat navigation between New York and New Jersey. However Gibbons, licensed under an Act of Congress, engaged in a coastal trade in New York waters, whereupon Ogden secured an injunction against Gibbons. The case finally came to the United States Supreme Court where Chief Justice Marshall speaking for the Court sustained the supremacy of the Act of Congress. In doing so he established three important elements of the Commerce Clause adjudicatory reference. Firstly he defined commerce broadly: 'Commerce undoubtedly, is traffic, but it is something more; it is intercourse. It describes the commercial intercourse between nations and parts of nations, in all its branches.'[28] Secondly he took an equally broad view of Congress's power to regulate commerce: 'What is this power? It is the power to regulate; that is, to prescribe the rule by which commerce is to be governed. This power, like all others vested in Congress is complete in itself, may be exercised to its utmost extent, and acknowledges no limitations, other than are prescribed in the constitution.'[29] But thirdly Marshall was very careful to establish that the power of Congress did not extend to commerce which was internal to a State: 'It is not intended to say that these words comprehend that commerce which is completely internal, which is carried on between man and man in a state, or between different parts of the same state, and which does not extend to or affect other states. Such a power would be inconvenient and is certainly unnecessary.'[30] Thus Marshall evolved a judicial formula which firstly accepted that commerce was more than goods. Secondly, the Congress could regulate the activities of interstate commerce in a variety of forms, but thirdly, it could not regulate commerce internal to a state. All three elements of this formula were not self-defining and were a source of litigation, but the third element was the most contentious and is particularly germane to the discussion of *Schechter*.

How did the courts distinguish between internal and interstate commerce? With difficulty, is a simple but fairly accurate answer. The problem that the courts faced was a lack of a readily-available formula which would provide a satisfactory rule for adjudication. The courts had to achieve a balance. The judiciary were obliged to ensure that commerce internal to a state remained outside of congressional jurisdiction. However, the identification of internal commerce was not a simple task because the character of the American economy by the late nineteenth century was changing. It was becoming complex, interdependent and national in outlook. Interstate commerce had long since passed the stage of goods crossing state boundaries. The judiciary were aware of these changes and, in the common law tradition, attempted to adapt legal rules to accommodate these developments. They did not, as is frequently alleged, refuse to recognise the new economic realities. For instance, in *Swift & Co.* v. *United States* the Supreme Court declared:

Commerce among the states is not a technical legal conception but a practical one, drawn from the course of business. When cattle are sent from a place in one State, with the expectation that they will end their transit, after purchase, in another, and when in effect they do so, with only the interruption necessary to find a purchaser at the stock yards, and when this is a typical, constantly recurring course, *the current thus existing is a current of commerce among the States . . .*'[31]

Similarly in *Stafford* v. *Wallace*, the Supreme Court after referring to 'modern economic conditions', went on to identify 'the great central fact that such *streams of commerce from one part of the country to another which are ever flowing* are in their very essence the commerce among the States and with foreign nations which historically it was one of the chief purposes of the Constitution to bring under national protection and control'.[32] Under the 'current of commerce' or 'streams of commerce' doctrine the Court was prepared to rule that certain forms of economic activity that took place entirely within a state nevertheless could be regulated by federal authority. In *Houston, E.&W. Texas Railroad* v. *United States*, also known as the *Shreveport Rate Case*, the United States Supreme Court allowed the Interstate Commerce Commission to set intrastate railroad rates alone. Interestingly the spokesman for the Court was Mr Justice Hughes in his first stint on the Court:

> The fact that carriers are instruments of intrastate commerce, as well as of interstate commerce, does not derogate from the complete and paramount authority of Congress over the latter or preclude the Federal power from being exerted to prevent the intrastate operations of such carriers from being made a means of injury to that which has been confined to Federal care . . . It is the Congress and not the State, that is entitled to prescribe the final and dominant rule, for otherwise Congress would be denied the exercise of its constitutional authority and the State, and not the Nation, would be supreme within the national field.[33]

Did the *Shreveport Rate Case* mean that the Congress had authority over commerce internal to a state? The answer was no, but the judiciary had shown in this case, plus *Swift* and *Stafford*, that it fully realised that there was no clear dividing line between interstate and intrastate commerce. The problem was that the courts faced a constitutional dividing line.

It was possible to argue, by the early twentieth century, that all commercial activities impinged, however minimally, on interstate commerce. If the courts had accepted this proposition, then the prohibition of Marshall in *Ogden* and subsequent judges would have been overruled. The Supreme Court was reluctant to do this and abandon the *Ogden* formula. Instead the Court attempted to give it life by using the idea of the direct versus the indirect effect on interstate commerce.[34] If intrastate commercial activities had a direct effect on interstate commerce then they fell within the jurisdiction of Congress, but if they had only an indirect effect, then they fell within the jurisdiction of the states. Of course, the direct–indirect rule was contentious, but it did permit the courts at one and the same time to recognise the economic realities of American industrial society, and to reaffirm the historically established limits to congressional power over commerce. It has been suggested that the direct–indirect rule was restrictive, if one could argue that the Congress's power over commerce should be unfettered. It certainly was not mechanical. Indeed it was a difficult rule to apply, and the implication that there was machinery which could easily locate commerce in one or two categories was entirely misplaced. Whether it was a satisfactory rule was another matter which the judiciary would consider at appropriate moments. But in 1935 it was the governing rule and Chief Justice Hughes applied it in *Schechter*. It was also a very appropriate rule for *Schechter*.

The government's fears that *Schechter* was an unhappy testcase for the National Industrial Recovery Act were borne out. The live poultry industry in New York was as localised as any industry could be. After the Schechter Corp. made its purchases of live poultry, all interstate transactions ended. They then took their poultry to 'their slaughterhouses in Brooklyn for local disposition ... they held their poultry at their slaughterhouse markets for slaughter and local sale to retail dealers and butchers who in turn sold directly to consumers. *Neither the slaughtering nor the sale by defendants were transactions in interstate commerce.*'[35] This did not end the matter as the practices of the live poultry industry could affect interstate commerce, in which case the Congress did have the authority to regulate the industry. The Chief Justice firstly established the reference of the argument: 'In determining how far the federal government may go in controlling interstate transactions upon the grounds that they "affect" interstate commerce, there is a necessary and well-established distinction between direct and indirect. *The precise line can be drawn only as individual cases arise, but the distinction is clear in principle.*[36] He then concluded, after an examination of the facts: 'The persons employed in slaughtering and selling in local trade are not employed in interstate commerce . . . and . . . have no direct relation to interstate commerce.' Justice Cardozo, in his concurring opinion similarly concluded that 'there is a view of causation that would obliterate the distinction between what is national and what is local in the activities of commerce . . . Activities local in their immediacy do not become interstate and national because of distant repercussions.'[37] The National Industrial Recovery Act was unconstitutional.

Yet again the Court's response to the New Deal was to evaluate the constitutionality of the contested legislation within a reference that was unanimously shared by all nine judges. But unlike *Railroad Retirement Board* and *Norman* v. *Baltimore and Ohio Railroad Co.*, the result in *Schechter* was also unanimous. The Court's unanimity in *Schechter* is clearly an embarrassment to those who attempt to explain the Court's response to the New Deal between 1934 and 1936 in terms of politics, social ideology and personal predilection. But unanimity *per se* is of no particular assistance to the explanation of the Court's position that is being suggested, and which will be fully articulated in Chapter 7. It does not particularly matter whether the Court was unanimous. What does matter are the reasons for the Court's unanimity. The reasons here were the shared reference for the evaluation of the Act's constitutionality and that legal rules played a crucial role in the creation of that reference. In some cases, indeed a great number of cases, judges will disagree while still agreeing about the reference, but the argument they conduct will be intelligible to all the participants. They will share the same language and will understand the reasons for disagreement even if they are bitterly expressed. In *Schechter* there was no dispute on the Court, because in 1935 the National Industrial Recovery Act crossed the permissible limits of legislative delegation and acceptable Commerce Clause regulation. It did not cross the line by an inch but by the constitutional equivalent of a mile. There was no possibility of the Court extending the boundaries to incorporate the NRA and its codes. But the important thing is that judges agreed that there was a boundary and they agreed on the process by which the Act could be placed within it or not.

## II

The Black Monday for the New Deal continued when the Frazier-Lemke Act[38] of 1934 was held, by a unanimous Court, to be unconstitutional in *Louisville Joint Stock Land Bank* v. *Radford*.[39] The Act was an amendment to the federal Bankruptcy Act which, like the Minnesota Mortgage Moratorium Law, was designed to relieve the widespread problem of foreclosures, although the Frazier-Lemke Act was restricted to farm foreclosures. The Roosevelt administration had not been entirely sympathetic to the bill, but since it had become law the Act had proven to be popular in agricultural communities.[40] The appeal of the Frazier-Lemke Act was that it offered assistance to farmers, again like the Minnesota Mortgage Moratorium Law, through modifying existing contracts between mortgagor and mortgagee. Thus in the event of a farmer defaulting on his repayments of capital and interest, he could declare himself bankrupt under Section 75 of the federal Bankruptcy Act and then seek relief under Paragraphs 3 and 7 of the Frazier-Lemke Act. This is precisely what Radford had done and indeed the facts of his case do illustrate the workings of the Act. In 1922 Radford mortgaged his farm worth $18,000 to the extent of $9,000 to the Louisville Joint Stock Land Bank. The mortgage was for thirty-four years and it attracted a rate of interest of 6 per cent. In 1932 and again in 1933 Radford defaulted on his repayments, and in June 1933 the bank foreclosed on Radford. Radford then decided to avail himself of the provisions under Section 75 of the Bankruptcy Act but could not convince a majority of his creditors to accept a composition of his debts, and on 30 June 1934 a state court ordered a foreclosure sale of his farm. But two days earlier on 28 June the Frazier-Lemke Act had been passed and Radford filed a petition before the state court claiming the relief provided in paragraphs 3 and 7 of the Frazier-Lemke Act.

Paragraphs 3 and 7 of the Act provided that, if the mortgagee should agree, then the mortgagor could purchase the property at its current appraisal value on the following terms. The mortgagor would acquire title and immediate possession. He would also agree to make deferred payments on a scale of '2½ per cent within two years; 2½ per cent within three years; 5 per cent within 4 years; 5 per cent within 5 years; the balance within six years. All deferred payments to bear interest at the rate of 1 per cent per annum.'[41] But in the event that the mortgagee refused to agree to this procedure the Frazier-Lemke Act set in motion the following alternative. The Act required the bankruptcy court to

> stay all proceedings for a period of five years, during which five years the debtors shall retain possession of all or any part of his property, . . . provided he pays a reasonable rental annually . . . At the end of five years the debtor may pay into court the appraisal price of the property of which he retains possession . . . and there-upon the court shall . . . turn over full possession and title of said property to the debtor and he may apply for his discharge as provided by the Act.[42]

Radford's petition was granted by the state court. His farm was appraised at $4,445, even though the bank offered $9,205.09, which was the amount outstanding on his debt. In any event the bank refused to agree to the first avenue provided under the Frazier-Lemke Act, i.e. the sale of the house to the debtor at the appraisal value. Thereupon the second alternative came into operation and all proceedings for the enforcement of the mortgage were stayed for five years. Radford was ordered to pay an annual rent of $325. The bank then challenged the constitutionality of the Frazier-Lemke Act in a suit in the federal court for Western Kentucky. The court held the statute valid as did the Circuit Court of Appeals. The case then arrived at the Supreme Court on a writ of certiorari.

The parlous financial condition of the agricultural community was undoubtedly the reason the Frazier-Lemke Act was proposed and passed. The proportionate size of mortgage indebtedness in relation to land value and farm income had increased and consequently caught farmers in a financial squeeze. But as with the Minnesota Mortgage Moratorium Law, Frazier-

Lemke's constitutionality depended on the mode of relief chosen by the authors of the Act rather than on their desire to help. Indeed the brief for Radford relied extensively on the holding in *Home Building and Loan Association* v. *Blaisdell*. In some respects the Frazier-Lemke Act appeared to be in a happier position than the Minnesota legislation. It did not, for instance, have to contend with the limitations of the contract clause. But there were other constitutional objections to the Act. The respondents in the case, the Louisville Joint Stock Land Bank, claimed that there were two substantial defects in the Act. Firstly, the bank charged, Frazier-Lemke was not a bankruptcy act. It disguised itself as such but it was legislation of a different ilk and thereby violated the Tenth Amendment of the Constitution. Secondly and more significantly, the brief for the respondents claimed to detect due process flaws in the Act. The opinion of the Court, written by Mr Justice Brandeis, evaluated these claims.

Justice Brandeis declined the opportunity to rule on the claim that the Frazier-Lemke Act was not a bankruptcy measure and thus avoided the substantive issue implicit in the claim of the extent of the powers of Congress under Article 1, Section 8 which declared that 'Congress shall have power . . . To establish uniform laws on the subject of Bankruptcies throughout the United States.' Nevertheless he observed that the Frazier-Lemke Act was certainly different to the bankruptcy measures that preceded it.

> The essential features of a bankruptcy law are these: the surrender by the debtor of his property . . . for distribution among his creditors . . . and the discharge by his creditors of all claims against the debtor; . . . on the other hand, the main purpose and the effect of the Frazier-Lemke Act is to prevent distribution of the farmer-mortgagor's property; to enable him to remain in possession despite persisting default; to scale down the mortgage debt; and to give the mortgagor the option to acquire the full title of the property upon paying the full amount.[43]

However, the fact that this Act differed from previous bankruptcy measures was not necessarily conclusive. 'But, the scope of the bankruptcy power conferred upon Congress is not necessarily limited to that which has been exercised.'[44] Clearly Brandeis wanted to avoid, and quite properly, an extensive discussion on the nature and extent of congressional power over bankruptcy and he could do so if the Act's constitutionality could be decided within the ambit of the Fifth Amendment and its due process clause.

The constitutional position post, *Blaisdell*, as the brief for Radford saw it, was that the Court would countenance abridgement of contract.[45] In *Blaisdell* the Court had sanctioned the action of a state government which had modified the contract between mortgagor and mortgagee to alleviate distress. The Frazier-Lemke Act in that respect was no different to the Minnesota Mortgage Moratorium Law. Admittedly, the Minnesota legislation had been an emergency measure but that aspect was only germane to the restrictions imposed by the contract clause, which of course did not apply to the federal government. Consequently the abridgement of contract that occurred under the Frazier-Lemke Act was also permissible. Undoubtedly the attorneys for Radford were making a case for their client but the quality of the argument betrayed a tendency towards what Mr Justice Harlan referred to as the 'domino theory' of adjudication.[46] Harlan's complaint was directed at his brethren for indiscriminately applying rules developed in Sixth Amendment cases to litigation concerning the Fifth Amendment. *Blaisdell* had been argued and decided within the confines of the contract clauses and the Chief Justice's opinion and that of Justice Sutherland addressed contract clause questions. The majority of the justices delineated certain limited possibilities for state governments to modify, temporarily, contracted obligations. The arguments and issues in *Blaisdell* did not have a great deal in common with those under consideration in *Louisville Joint Stock Land Bank* v. *Radford*. Nevertheless was it not possible to argue that in *Blaisdell* the Court had established a permissive attitude towards contractual obligation? If so, *Blaisdell* was germane to the issues under consideration in *Radford*.

The answer to the question was that the Court in *Blaisdell* did not strike an attitude toward contractual obligation. It made a decision which permitted a state government to modify contractual obligations and in order to do so it formulated a rule. This rule, as has been suggested above, was not a great departure from previous practice, because while it sustained the Minnesota legislation, it also re-established restrictions on the use of state power. It did not discard the contract clause; the rule reasserted its protections. Hughes' opinion did not contain a permissive attitude to state power; instead it sought to achieve a delicate balance between state authority and constitutional limitations. The *Blaisdell* rule exuded a sense of complexity and subtlety which does not permit itself to be described as revealing an attitude. Hughes was too sophisticated a jurist for such a claim to be convincing. In any case the record of the Court post-*Blaisdell* is also proof that there was no simple attitude at the core of the *Blaisdell* rule. In *Worthen Co.* v. *Thomas*[47] a unanimous Court held an Arkansas statute which modified contractual obligations, to be unconstitutional. Similarly in *Worthen Co.* v. *Kavanaugh*[48] another Arkansas law which reduced the remedies in foreclosure proceedings was also unanimously held to be invalid. *Blaisdell* did not offer a *carte blanche* to state governments over contractual obligations.[49]

On what basis did the Supreme Court distinguish between the Minnesota Mortgage Moratorium Law and the two Arkansas statutes mentioned above? Under the Minnesota law, in the event of default the period of redemption from foreclosure sales was extended for a maximum of two years and the extension was granted only under judicial supervision. Furthermore the state courts were required to determine the 'reasonable value of the income of the property involved in the sale, or if it has no income, then the reasonable value of the property, and direct the mortgagor to pay all or a reasonable part of such income or rental value in or toward the payment of taxes, interest, mortgage'.[50] At the end of the extension, the mortgagee was free to foreclose if there was no mutually acceptable arrangement. So the rights of the mortgagee, under the Minnesota law, were not lessened or reduced. They were put into abeyance and the mortgagee received compensation for the delay in executing his entitlement. But in *Worthen* v. *Kavanaugh*, the Court accused the State of Arkansas of 'studied indifference to the mortgagee and to his appropriate protection'.[51] Could the same accusation be levelled at the Frazier-Lemke Act?

When Mr Justice Brandeis commenced his evaluation of the claim that the Frazier-Lemke Act violated the due process of law, he accepted that the Congress had the authority to discharge the obligations of debtors. However, as he pointed out, the complaint concerning the Act was not 'the discharge of Radford's obligations. It is the taking of substantive rights in specific property acquired by the Bank prior to the Act.'[52] And so Brandeis noted there were certainly various unique features to the Act: 'No instance had been found, except under the Frazier-Lemke Act, of either a statute or decision compelling the mortgagee to relinquish the property to the mortgagor free of the lien unless the debt was paid in full.'[53] Again Brandeis observed: 'Although each of our national bankruptcy acts followed a major or minor depression, none had, prior to the Frazier-Lemke Act, sought to compel the holder of a mortgage to surrender to the bankrupt either the possession of the title or the mortgaged property of the title so long as any part of the debt ... remained unpaid.'[54]

But Brandeis did not find that these novel features by themselves warranted the Act being declared unconstitutional. The Act's unconstitutionality ultimately depended on whether the bank had suffered a substantive loss of property rights through these features. Thus Brandeis had to establish what the rights of a mortgagee were before the Frazier-Lemke Act was passed. In order to do so he had to establish the bank's position pre-Frazier-Lemke in Kentucky Law. Having done so, Brandeis listed the loss of property rights suffered by the Bank:

1 The right to retain the lien until the indebtedness thereby secured is paid.
2 The right to realize upon the security by a judicial public sale.
3 The right to determine when such a sale shall be held, subject only to the discretion of the court.
4 The right to protect its interest in the property by bidding at such a sale ... and thus to assure having the mortgaged property devoted primarily to the satisfaction of the debt, either through receipt of the proceeds of a fair competitive sale or by taking the property itself.
5 The right to control meanwhile the property during the period of default, subject only to the discretion of the court, and to have the rents and profits collected ... for the satisfaction of the debt.[55]

The Frazier-Lemke Act had not put the mortgagee's rights

into abeyance; it had rewritten and, more significantly, reduced them. Moreover the Congress was fully aware of the reduction in the mortgagee's rights. When the Congress debated whether the Frazier-Lemke Act should apply to new mortgages as well as to existing mortgages, both Senators and Representatives forcefully pointed out the folly of any such move. Farmers, they agreed, would find it all but impossible to raise new mortgage finance, if the reduction in the mortgagee's rights, imposed under the Act, were to apply to new mortgages.[56] As a result of these warnings the Frazier-Lemke Act only applied to existing mortgages as Congress fully realised that the reduction in the mortgagee's rights were so substantial that there could be a considerable difficulty in raising new mortgage finance if the Act was applied to new mortgages. The Court also shared Congress's judgement on the loss of the mortgagee's property rights. As Brandeis phrased it, 'the Frazier-Lemke Act as applied has taken from the Bank without compensation and given to Radford rights in property which are of substantial value . . . We must hold it [the act] void.'[57]

Radford had one further claim that even if the mortgagee's rights had been substantially reduced, it was done for the public good. Public policy, Radford claimed, required individually owned and operated farms, and this policy was in jeopardy with the extent of foreclosures that were taking place. Brandeis responded: 'The Fifth Amendment commands that however great the Nation's need, private property shall not thus be taken even for a wholly public use without just compensation.'[58] He concluded with a word of advice for the federal government: 'If the public interest requires, and permits, the taking of property of individual mortgagees in order to relieve the necessities of individual mortgagors resort must be had to proceedings by eminent domain; so that, through taxation, the burden of the relief afforded in the public interest may be borne by the public.'[59]

*Louisville Joint Stock Land Bank* v. *Radford* was probably the least controversial of the New Deal cases. The defects in the Frazier-Lemke Act were apparent and noted by legislators in Congress. Brandeis's opinion followed the well established reference and context for the evaluation due process claims, which made it difficult to criticise. There was nothing even mildly wayward or idiosyncratic about Brandeis's opinion. Indeed the only mildly surprising element in the litigation over the Frazier-Lemke Act was that it had been sustained in the lower federal courts. Indeed Homer Cummings, the Attorney General, observed that eleven judges, six circuit court judges and five district court judges had voted to sustain the Act while a total of eleven judges, none on the Supreme Court, plus two district court judges had voted against the Act being constitutional. Cummings was reported to have said 'sarcastically to Roosevelt, 'Manifestly the law is an exact science.'[60] Of course the law is not exact nor is it a science, although it would be interesting to know what paradigm of science Cummings had in mind. Nevertheless it is clear from the New Deal cases which came before the Court between 1934 and 1936 that the nine judges were not applying the exact rules of a scientific discipline. The Court was involved in constitutional interpretation and constitutional interpretation is an imprecise art. It is subject to disagreement and open to argument. But it is not a formless process where judges may do as they please. Quite to the contrary the legal process has a highly structured form. Judges operate within a set of agreed rules and mutually accepted concepts of reasoning and argument and these formal elements are absolutely crucial in shaping the judicial decision, or at least that was the position on the Supreme Court in the 1930s and *Radford* is evidence of it.

**NOTES**

1 *Humphrey's Executor* v. *United States*, 295 US 602 (1935).
2 *Louisville Bank* v. *Radford*, 295 US 555 (1935).
3 *A. L. A. Schechter Poultry Corp. et al.* v. *United States*, 295 US 490 (1935).
4 E. Hawley, *The New Deal and the Problem of Monopoly* (1966), p. 130.
5 *New York Times*, 30 May 1935.
6 E. Gerhart, *American's Advocate: Robert H. Jackson* (1958), p. 99.
7 B. Rauch (ed.), *Franklin D. Roosevelt: Selected Speeches, Messages, Press Conferences and Letters* (1964), pp. 171–81.
8 A. Schlesinger, Jr, *The Coming of the New Deal* (1958), p. 118.
9 See H. Johnson, *The Blue Eagle from Egg to Earth* (1935); R. Moley, *After Seven Years* (1939).
10 H. Johnson, *The Blue Eagle*, note 9, p. 193.
11 See Title I of the National Industrial Recovery Act, 48 Stat. 195.
12 E. Hawley, *New Deal*, note 4, pp. 33, 34.
13 294 US 736 (1935).
14 R. Jackson, *The Struggle for Judicial Supremacy* (1941), p. 113.
15 *New York Herald Tribune*, 3 April 1935.

16 The full title of the Code was 'Code of Fair Competition for the Live Poultry Industry of the Metropolitan Area in and out the City of New York'.
17 Executive Order No. 6892 dated 13 April 1934.
18 295 US 495, 516 (1935).
19 Quoted in W. Letwin, *Law and Economic Policy in America* (1967), p. 277.
20 295 US 495, 533 (1935).
21 *Ibid.*, p. 517.
22 48 Stat. 195.
23 295 US 495, 551 (1935).
24 *Ibid.*, pp. 541, 542.
25 *Ibid.*, p. 553.
26 9 Wheat. 1 (1824).
27 S. F. Miller, *Lectures on the Constitution* (1893), p. 433.
28 9 Wheat. 1, 189, 190 (1824).
29 *Ibid.*, pp. 196, 197.
30 *Ibid.*, p. 194.
31 196 US 375, 398, 399 (1905) (emphasis added).
32 258 US 495, 518, 519 (1922) (emphasis added).
33 234 US 342, 351, 352 (1914).
34 The doctrine is claimed to have emerged in *United States* v. *E. C. Knight Co.*, 156 US 1 (1895). See also *Adair* v. *United States*, 208 US 161 (1908); *Hammer* v. *Dagenhart*, 247 US 251 (1918).
35 295 US 495, 543 (1935) (emphasis added).
36 *Ibid.*, p. 546 (emphasis added).
37 Ibid., p. 544.
38 48 Stat. 1289.
39 295 US 555 (1935).
40 C. Leonard, *A Search for a Judicial Philosophy: Mr Justice Roberts and the Constitutional Revolution of 1937* (1971), p. 57. See also B. Rauch, *The History of the New Deal* (1963), p. 119.
41 295 US 555, 574 (1935).
42 *Ibid.*, pp. 575, 576.
43 *Ibid.*, p. 586.
44 *Ibid.*, p. 587.
45 *Ibid.*, pp. 562–70.
46 See the dissenting opinion of Harlan J. in *Miranda* v. *Arizona*, 384 US 436, 514 (1966).
47 292 US 426 (1934).
48 295 US 56 (1935).
49 See *Triegle* v. *Acme Homestead Association*, 279 US 189 (1936).
50 290 US 398, 416, 417 (1934).
51 295 US 56 (1935).
52 295 US 555, 580, 581 (1935).
53 *Ibid.*, p. 579.
54 *Ibid.*, pp. 581, 582.
55 *Ibid.*, pp. 594, 595.
56 *Congressional Record* (1934), pp. 12074–137.
57 295 US 555, 601 (1935).
58 *Ibid.*, p. 602.
59 *Ibid.*, p. 602.
60 Quoted in A. Schlesinger Jr, *Politics of Upheaval* (1966), p. 280.

# 6

# The New Deal in Court III: agriculture and coal

I

The last two important New Deal Cases[1] that were decided before the 'constitutional revolution'[2] of 1937 concerned the Agricultural Adjustment Act of 1933[3] and the Bituminous Coal Conservation Act of 1935.[4] In both cases, *United States* v. *Butler et al.*[5] and *Carter* v. *Carter Coal,*[6] the Court was divided closely but decisively against the New Deal measures. They were controversial decisions and perhaps the controversy engendered by the two cases as well as the subsequent case, *Morehead* v. *New York ex rel. Tipaldo,*[7] convinced President Roosevelt to proceed with his plans to 'pack' the Court.[8] But whereas *Morehead*, which concerned the constitutionality of a New York statute fixing the wages for women, did not cause the Roosevelt administration any discomfort but merely furnished the opportunity to proceed against the Court, both the *Butler* and *Carter* cases did cause serious political problems for the administration. The Agricultural Adjustment Act, in particular, had been one of the political success stories of the New Deal. It was popular among farmers and its popularity was well deserved for the Act had brought about a considerable transfer of income from the non-agricultural sector into farming. The farmers' organisations and the political representatives of the farm states had attempted to achieve this objective throughout the 1920s but with meagre success. Consequently they were very grateful to President Roosevelt and their gratitude was graphically expressed in the presidential election of 1936.

Farmers were anxious for government involvement in agriculture during the 1920s because the economic depression that struck industrial America at the end of the 1920s had reached the agricultural economy a decade earlier. In 1919, gross farm income was $16·9 billion but the sum was almost halved by 1921. In 1925 income had recovered to $11·9 billion but that figure was the high point for the decade. The reason for this sharp decline in income was readily identifiable. It was over-production. Agricultural production had been increased during World War I to cope with the vastly increased demand for American agricultural produce. But when the demand abruptly declined after the end of the war, production was not reduced commensurately. Consequently a disequilibrium between supply and demand emerged, a disequilibrium which was reinforced by the increasing productivity of the American farmer. Thus agriculture throughout the 1920s was faced with the problem of chronic oversupply.[9] As Rexford Tugwell wrote: 'The Malthusian thesis of a population pressing upon the food supply has become for the time being, at least, a food supply pressing upon the population. The Malthusians feared scarcity . . . Yet in our generation we have seen scarcity vanquished, and our ever present fear, so far as agriculture is concerned, is a fear of over-abundance.'[10] The problem with 'over-abundance', of course, was severely depressed price levels.

The response of the farmers, through their numerous organisations and their political representatives, to the depressed prices for agricultural commodities was to involve the federal government in a programme to raise prices. The vehicle they adopted in the 1920s to achieve their objective with varying degrees of enthusiasm was known as McNary-Haugenism.[11] Four McNary-Haugen bills were introduced during the decade, two of which were passed by the Congress only to be vetoed by President Coolidge. The idea behind the bills, in the words of the biographer of George Peek who was, with Hugh Johnson, the driving force behind McNary-Haugenism, was 'to restore and maintain ratio-prices for basic farm commodities by establishing a government corporation with power to buy and dispose of surpluses.'[12] Peek and Johnson wanted the federal government to establish a ratio-price between agricultural and industrial commodities derived from price indices in the period 1905–41, when they believed a 'fair' and 'appropriate' relationship existed between the prices for agricultural and industrial products. After the government had established the ratio-price for each of the specific farm commodities covered by the bill, and the number of commodities varied between the four McNary-Haugen bills, Peek and Johnson wanted the federal government to guarantee that the market price never fell below the designated ratio-price, by purchasing the requisite amount of the designated commodities to ensure the objective. The government would then sell the commodities it had purchased on the world market. Another feature of the McNary-Haugen bills was a flexible tariff provision to prevent foreign produce undercutting the ratio-price.[13] It was an attractive scheme for farmers, particularly for those who grew wheat and cotton and were being severely affected by the steep decline in demand. Unfortunately it was a scheme which had many obvious weaknesses.

McNary-Haugenism had two crucial defects. As Van Perkins noted:

> The shortcoming of McNary-Haugenism bothered an increasing number of people who, while friendly to the idea of government action to provide farm relief, were increasingly doubtful about the practicability of the . . . scheme. One of the doubts related to whether or not exports could be dumped abroad . . . in the face of increasing tariffs and other devices being employed by other nations to keep agricultural imports out . . . Another doubt related to the effect of the program on production. Most observers were convinced that higher prices would stimulate production and they argued that higher production would make the program ineffective.[14]

These doubts were persuasive. Higher prices would almost certainly stimulate high production which would be self-defeating for farmers. Furthermore, it was most unlikely that other countries which had an export trade in agricultural products would accept the United States dumping its surpluses on the world market. Fortunately there was a suggestion available which could resolve both problems.

Clearly if the federal government was going to guarantee a minimum price for a range of farm commodities, it also had to have a measure of control over production. Otherwise its financial commitment to ensure that the market price never fell below the guaranteed price would be defined not by government, but by individual farmers when they made their decisions over the levels of their own production. Most administrations of both political parties would find this a rather unattractive proposition. Furthermore, although production controls would not obviate the need for the federal government to intervene in the commodity markets, the controls ought to prevent overly large surpluses from emerging and consequently spare the federal government the embarrassment of dumping the surpluses on the world markets. Unfortunately, the mechanisms to control production were not easy to devise and few acceptable suggestions emerged until the development of Domestic Allotment. The idea of Domestic Allotment was proposed initially by W. J. Spillman in 1927 but the name most clearly associated with it is M. L. Wilson. It was Wilson who convinced Roosevelt's 'Brain Trust' of the advantages of Domestic Allotment, but that story has been told elsewhere.[15] The bare outline of Domestic Allotment was that if a farmer voluntarily accepted a reduction in his acreage, i.e. if he agreed to reduce the number of acres he cultivated, then he would receive a benefit payment from the federal government. The government would raise the revenue for this benefit payment by imposing an excise tax on the processing of the commodity. The Domestic Allotment idea was both simple and ingenious; it was also central to the Agricultural Adjustment Act.

On 10 March 1933 there was a conference at the Department of Agriculture in Washington. The leaders of the main four organisations attended and when they emerged from the conference, with one exception, they endorsed the principles behind the Act.[16] The aim of the Act was to raise the market price for corn, cotton, wheat, tobacco and rice to the McNary-Haugen ratio-price, except that this was now known as the parity price or parity.[17] The parity price would be the equivalent of the price that these commodities had fetched between August 1909 and July 1914, which in the Act's opinion was a period when a 'fair exchange value' existed between farm and non-farm products.[18] In order to achieve this objective, an Agricultural Adjustment Administration was established and its task was to enter into voluntary agreements with farmers to reduce the acreage they cultivated on a basis related to the average acreage that had been under cultivation in the previous five years. In return for their co-operation farmers received a benefit payment.[19] These payments were to be funded by a tax on the first domestic processing of the commodity. The Act also contained a tax on floor stocks, which applied to commodities which had been processed before the imposition of a processing tax, and a tax on 'competing products' both domestic and foreign.[20] Under the Act, the Secretary of Agriculture was authorised to enter into marketing agreements 'with processors, associations of producers . . . and others engaged in the handling . . . of any agricultural commodity or product'.[21] Furthermore, the Secretary had the authority to issue licences to them, and without these licences they could not handle agricultural commodities.[22] All of the above provisions were contained in Title I, which was the heart of the Agricultural Adjustment Act. This Act, unlike the National Industrial Recovery Act, embodied ideas that had been discussed publicly and widely over the previous decade. The notion of parity price and production control were well known in Washington by 1933. Nevertheless when they were given legislative effect on 12 May 1933 the Roosevelt administration was about to embark on what could only be considered a novel experiment in government.

> In one sense the Agricultural Adjustment Act was neither new nor revolutionary: it drew heavily on the ideas which had been advanced in the twenties and early thirties . . . there was much of McNary-Haugenism of . . . domestic allotment . . . in it. But, in the extent of governmental intervention it contemplated, and in the administrative flexibility it permitted, it was indeed a new and untrod path for American agriculture and for the American government.[23]

Perhaps it was the 'untrod path' that aroused doubts about the Act's constitutionality, but questions were asked and most of them were directed at the propriety of the processing tax.

In the two-and-a-half years after the passage of the Agricultural Adjustment Act, over 1,700 injunctions had been requested from the courts to restrain the collection of the processing tax and the tax was also the bone of contention in *United States* v. *Butler et al.* The facts in *Butler* were as follows. The receivers of the Hoosac Mills Corp. had received a claim for processing and floor taxes on cotton. The receivers had refused to pay, whereupon they were sued by the government. The District Court found the taxes valid and ordered them to be paid, but when the receivers appealed the Circuit Court of Appeals reversed the order. The case arrived at the Supreme Court on a writ of certiorari. On 9 December 1935 oral arguments commenced before the Court and over 2,000 people tried to attend. Those that did get in saw, according to *Newsweek*, the Solicitor General, Stanley Reed, 'blanch and sway' from the questions that the Justices threw at him.[24] They also heard George Wharton Pepper, counsel for the receivers of Hoosac Mills Corp., offer his prayer: 'I pray Almighty God that not in my time may "the land of the regimented" be accepted as a worthy substitute for the "land of the free".'[25] The atmosphere was apparently no less charged when Roberts read the opinion of the Court on 6 January 1936:

> An overflow crowd filled every seat in the ornate classical audi-
> torium as Justice Roberts, in the hush of expectancy, began to
> deliver the opinion of six members of the Court ... The most
> accomplished member of the Court in the histrionics of adjudi-
> cation, Roberts spoke his opinions as from memory, hardly glanc-
> ing at the printed pages on the mahogany desk before him, domi-
> nating the room with the confident resonance of his voice, his
> rugged head and powerful frame rendered particularly impressive
> by the flow of black judicial robes.[26]

But whether Roberts' judgement justified the sense of high drama in the courtroom was questionable.

Roberts' opinion hinged on a determination of fact. Was the processing tax a tax? Was it like any other general revenue measure or was it, in fact, part of a regulation of an activity, i.e. agriculture, which was not necessarily within the jurisdiction of the federal government? The answer to these questions would determine Roberts' response to a series of claims including the very right of the respondents to question the validity of the Agricultural Adjustment Act. In their brief, the government had argued that under the doctrine enunciated in *Massachusetts* v. *Mellon*,[27] the receivers of the Hoosac Mills Corp. had no standing in the *Butler* case. For in *Massachusetts* v. *Mellon* the Supreme Court, through an opinion by Mr Justice Sutherland, had declared that the constitutionality of an Act of Congress could only be challenged if there was a

> direct injury suffered or threatened, presenting a justiciable
> issue ... The party ... must be able to show not only that the
> statute is invalid, but that he has sustained or is immediately in
> danger of sustaining some direct injury as the result of its enforce-
> ment, and not merely that he suffers in some indefinite way in
> common with people generally.[28]

But, Sutherland continued, with reference to revenue laws, the
interest in the individual tax payer 'in the moneys of the Treasury
... is shared with millions of others and is comparatively minute
and indeterminable and remote, ... that no basis is afforded for
an appeal ... to a court'.[29] Thus if the processing tax was a
revenue measure then the respondents had no standing in *Butler*.
But that, of course, begged the question.

If the processing tax was not a tax and the Court perceived it
along with the benefit payments to farmers as the inextricably
linked elements of one and the same regulation to control
agricultural production, then there were doubts over the constitutionality of the Agricultural Adjustment Act, because the federal
government was then using its taxing and spending power to
regulate an industry which it perhaps was not constitutionally
entitled to regulate. But if the processing tax was indeed a revenue
measure, then the Court could legitimately treat it, and the benefit
payments, as separate entities, which would almost certainly lead to
the conclusion that the Act was constitutional. For there was no
disagreement on the Court that the Congress had the authority to
levy a tax on the processing of agricultural commodities. The nine
judges were as one in their belief that the federal government,
under the taxing power, had the right to impose such a tax. There
was also no reason to believe that any member of the Court
believed that the benefit payments were an unconstitutional
exercise of the spending power, although interestingly the government brief expected this to be a major point of contention.

The first sentence of Article 1 Section 8 of the Constitution is
as follows: 'The Congress shall have Power to lay and collect Taxes,
Duties, Imposts and Excises, to pay the Debts and provide for the
common Defence and general welfare of the United States.' The
words are clear and explicit with one exception. What did the

words, 'provide for . . . the general welfare' mean? Did the words, known as the general welfare clause, imply a limitation on the taxing and spending power, and how extensive was the limitation? The government brief attempted to provide an answer. It suggested that there were two broad streams of interpretation. One was suggested by James Madison, the other by Alexander Hamilton.

> It is said that the general welfare clause is a limitation on the taxing power; that the clause itself has reference to and is limited by subsequently enumerated powers; that is, that Congress can tax only to carry out one or more of these latter powers. This is known as the Madisonian theory . . . It is said that while the clause is a limitation on the taxing and spending power, it was intended to embrace objects beyond those included in the subsequently enumerated powers; that is that although Congress may not accomplish the general welfare independently of the taxing power, nevertheless it may tax (and spend) in order to promote the national welfare by means which may not be within the scope of other Congressional powers. This is commonly known as the Hamiltonian theory.[30]

The strategy of the government brief was clear. It wished to demonstrate that the Hamiltonian interpretation was correct, for if the Court adopted the conception put forward by Madison, that the taxing and spending power was limited by the general welfare clause to those enumerated powers listed in the subsequent clauses in Article 1 Section 8, then the powers of the federal government to tax and to appropriate would be severely restricted. The brief, however, marshalled its arguments ably and demonstrated skillfully that the overwhelming weight of historical, legal and constitutional opinion supported the Hamiltonian interpretation, that Congress did have a substantive power to tax, admittedly limited by the general welfare clause, but that this limitation was distinct from the enumerated powers in Article 1 Section 8. Mr Justice Roberts did not dissent from the government's conclusion. He agreed with their contention, possibly because of the brief's persuasiveness, although it is much more likely that Roberts' agreement was the result of Hamilton's ideas having being accepted *de facto* for some considerable time. In any case he dismissed the Madisonian interpretation of the general welfare clause as a 'mere tautology'[31] and observed that Justice Story in his *Commentaries on the Constitution of the United States*[32] supported Hamilton's position

> Study . . . leads us to conclude that the reading advocated by Mr Justice Story is the correct one. While, therefore, the power to tax is not unlimited, its confines are set in the clause which confers it, and not in those of Section 8 which bestow and define the power of Congress. It results that the power of Congress to authorize expenditure of public moneys for public purposes is not limited by the direct grants of legislative power found in the constitution.[33]

Thus Roberts accepted that the taxing and spending power of Congress was limited by a general welfare clause that transcended the specific grants of power listed in Article 1 Section 8. Of course even Story and Hamilton believed that the general welfare clause imposed limitations on the taxing and spending power, but their definition of the clause provided the Congress with a greater latitude. By 1933 this greater latitude would have enabled the Congress to finance the benefit payments.[34] It would also have sanctioned the Congress's decision to levy a tax on the processing of agricultural commodities as long as it was a genuine revenue measure; but was it?

Mr Justice Roberts had little doubt of the nature of the processing tax.

> The tax can only be sustained by ignoring the avowed purpose and operation of the act, and holding it a measure merely laying an excise upon processors to raise revenue for the support of government. Beyond cavil the sole objective of the legislation is to restore the purchasing power of agricultural products to . . . parity; to take money from the processors and bestow it upon farmers who will reduce their acreage . . . It is inaccurate and misleading to speak of the exaction . . . as a tax.[35]

Several consequences flowed from Roberts' determination that the processing tax was not a tax. Firstly, the receivers of the Hoosac Mills Corp. did have standing in *Butler* and could challenge the constitutionality of the Agricultural Adjustment Act. Secondly, Roberts had then to establish the true nature of the processing tax. If it was not a revenue tax, what was it?

113

'The statute . . . by its operation shows the exaction laid upon processors to be the necessary means for the intended control of agricultural products.'[36] Thus, according to Roberts, the processing tax and indeed the benefit payments[37] were devices in an overall legislative plan to control agricultural production. If the Congress wished to regulate agricultural production, then it would have to establish a constitutional authority to do so, independent of the taxing power, for the Supreme Court, in the preceding decade, had reaffirmed its long-standing prohibition[38] on the Congress from regulating matters by taxation over which it had no jurisdiction. In *Bailey* v. *Drexel Furniture Co.*,[39] usually known as the Child Labor Tax Case, the Court ruled that an Act of Congress, which imposed a 10 per cent tax on the profits of all persons employing children, was unconstitutional. Chief Justice Taft spoke for the majority, including Justices Brandeis and Holmes, when he declared: 'The so-called tax is a penalty to coerce people of a State to act as Congress wishes them to act in respect of a matter completely the business of the state government under the Federal Constitution.'[40] On the same day as the Child Labor Tax Case was decided the Court, again through Taft, ruled that the Congress had used the taxing power improperly in the Grain Futures Trading Act. The tax imposed in the Act, Taft argued, was not a revenue measure but a method of controlling the boards of trade, whose behaviour the Congress had not entitlement to control.[41] In *United States* v. *Constantine*[42] which also validated an Act of Congress on the same grounds, Mr Justice Roberts declared: 'If in reality a tax is a penalty it cannot be converted into a tax by so naming it, and we must ascribe to it the character disclosed by its purpose and operation, regardless of name . . . it is a penalty for the violation of state law and as such beyond the limits of federal power.'[43] Thus the question was: did Congress have the constitutional authority to control agricultural production?

Roberts framed his reply to the question in the following manner:

> From the accepted doctrine that the United States is a government of delegated powers, it follows that those not expressly granted, or reasonably to be implied from such as are conferred, are reserved to the states or to the people. To forestall any suggestion to the

contrary, the Tenth Amendment was adopted. The same proposition, otherwise stated, is that powers not granted are prohibited. None to regulate agricultural production is given and therefore legislation by Congress for that purpose is forbidden.'[44]

Roberts did not elaborate any further on this point. Although it is surprising that an issue of importance should be disposed of in a few sentences, it is nevertheless interesting to note that the government brief did not make any claim that the Congress had the authority to regulate agricultural production. The brief had studiously avoided any attempt to justify the validity of the Agricultural Adjustment Act on Commerce Clause or indeed any other grounds, bar the taxing power.[45] Even more significantly, the dissenting opinion of Mr Justice Stone did not take issue with this particular point in Roberts' opinion.

Roberts concluded his judgement by dismissing the government's final contention that the Agricultural Adjustment Act was based on a voluntary agreement between the farmer and the federal government.

> The regulation is not . . . voluntary. The farmer, of course, may refuse to comply, but the price of such refusal is the loss of benefits. The amount offered is intended to be sufficient to exert pressure on him to agree to the proposed regulation. The power to confer or withhold unlimited benefits is the power to coerce or destroy. If the cotton grower elects not to accept the benefits he will receive less for his crops; those who receive payments will be able to undersell him. The result may well be financial ruin . . . This is coercion by economic pressure. The asserted power of choice is illusory.[46]

This was perhaps the most awkward passage in Roberts' opinion. He appeared to be arguing that the government could not offer a grant of money with attached conditions for that was tantamount to coercing those persons who did not approve of the conditions but could not resist the lure of the money. This presented a tempting target to Stone who could not resist the opportunity for ridicule: 'The limitation . . . must lead to absurd consequences. The government may give seeds to farmers but may not condition the gift upon their being planted . . . It may give money to sufferers from earthquake, fire, tornado, pestilence or flood but may not impose conditions – health precautions designed to prevent the spread of disease . . .[47] But Roberts was, in fact, saying something slightly different which developed as a consequence of his determination on the nature of the processing tax. Just as the processing tax was not a revenue measure, so the benefit payments were not a spending measure. The processing tax was a device to raise money in order to fund the benefit payments to farmers who on receipt of the payment would reduce their output. The tax and the payment were inextricably linked elements of a federal regulation to control agricultural production, which was unconstitutional. The power to tax and spend could not be exercised in the attainment of an objective that was unconstitutional, and the Congress could not elude this limitation by creating a programme based on voluntary agreements, which contained conditions that gave effect to objectives that the Congress had no entitlement to impose, especially when the voluntary agreement was given, as Roberts noted, in circumstances where the alternative was 'financial ruin' Of course, where the power of the Congress to tax and appropriate was used constitutionally, Roberts did not deny the Congress's authority to impose conditions on the acceptance of federal money. He could not have done so as the practice was too well established.[48]

In summary, Roberts accepted the Hamilton–Story version of the taxing power and the general welfare clause. Therefore he accepted that the Congress could levy an excise tax on the processing of agricultural products as long as it was a revenue measure. But Roberts claimed that the tax was not a revenue measure, and along with the benefit payments was a federal attempt to regulate agricultural production, which was not within the jurisdiction of the federal government. Consequently the Agricultural Adjustment Act was unconstitutional, a state which could not be redeemed by the so-called voluntary nature of the agreements between the farmer and the federal government. Justice Stone, along with Justices Brandeis and Cardozo, dissented. Where did Stone disagree with Roberts? In his opinion he also accepted the Hamilton/Story interpretation and the congressional right to levy a processing tax on agricultural production. At this point, however, he departed from the holding in the majority opinion. In Stone's assessment the processing tax was a revenue measure and the consequences of his assessment led him to very different conclusions. The tax and the benefit payments could be viewed as two separate entities. They were a revenue and an appropriation measure respectively, and were authorised by the taxing and spending power in Article 1 Section 8. The Congress, as with any legitimate exercise of that power, could impose conditions on the spending of federal money and therefore the benefit payments with its conditions did not pose any constitutional problems. Therefore, Stone felt that the Agricultural Adjustment Act did not regulate agricultural production, an activity which he implicitly accepted was constitutionally barred to the federal government, but was an exercise of the taxing power and as such was constitutional. Both opinions, Roberts' and Stone's, turned on their very different answer to the same question. What was the true nature of the processing tax? They did not disagree about the law, they differed on the determination of fact. Why then did they differ on this point? Why did Stone see the processing tax in a very different light to Roberts?

It is interesting that Stone's discussion of the nature of the tax was brief. He disposed of the problem swiftly. He did not embark on an extended discussion of the characteristics of a revenue measure; instead he dealt with the subject almost hastily:

> The constitutional power of Congress to levy an excise tax upon the processing of agricultural products is not questioned. The present levy is held invalid . . . because . . . it is a step in a plan to regulate agricultural production and is thus a forbidden infringement of state. The levy is not any less an exercise of taxing power because it is intended to defray an expenditure for the general welfare than for some other support of government.[49]

Thus in Stone's assessment the benefit payments were authorised by Congress's duty to 'provide for the . . . general welfare' and the processing tax was an excise tax. The proceeds from the tax went towards the cost of the benefit payments and that was the extent of the link between the processing tax and the benefit payments. But why did Stone believe this rather than Roberts' version of the relationship between tax and payment? The answer was never made completely explicit, but Stone's entire opinion exuded a quality which is known as judicial self-restraint. It is a quality which made Stone reluctant to share Roberts' interpretation of events. As Stone perceived the position, the Congress had the right to impose an excise tax on the processing of agricultural produce. In the Agricultural Adjustment Act, Congress declared that it had imposed such a tax and the tax had all the overt indications of being a revenue measure. Thus there was no need to press the examination of the processing tax any further. Congress ought to be believed and judges, as Stone suggested, ought to restrain themselves from evaluating the constitutionality of actions, taken by the political branches of government: 'While the unconstitutional exercise of power by the executive and legislative branches of the government is subject to judicial restraint, the only check upon our own exercise of power is our own sense of self-restraint.'[50] Stone's plea was not idiosyncratic. Self-restraint was a notion that had found expression on the Court on numerous occasions.

In *Fletcher* v. *Peck*, Chief Justice John Marshall wrote: 'The question, whether a law be void for repugnancy to the constitution, is, at all times a question of much delicacy, which ought seldom, if ever, to be decided in the affirmative in a doubtful case.' Sixty years later Chief Justice Waite reiterated the same sentiments.[51] 'Every statute is presumed to be constitutional. The Courts ought not to declare one to be unconstitutional unless it is clearly so. If there is doubt, the express will of the legislative should be sustained.'[52] Waite then articulated another element contained within the idea of self-restraint: 'For protection against abuses by legislatures the people must resort to the polls not the courts.'[53] This theme was elaborated on by Justice Frankfurter in the first of the legislative apportionment cases, *Baker* v. *Carr*.[54] Frankfurter claimed that there ought to be:

> a frank acknowledgement that there is not under our Constitution a judicial remedy for every political mischief, for every undesirable exercise of legislative power. In this situation as in others . . . relief does not belong here. Appeal must be to an informed civically militant electorate. In a democratic society like ours relief must come through an aroused popular conscience that sears the conscience of the people's representatives.[55]

These passages contain the essence of the notion of judicial self-restraint. Firstly, the judiciary ought to respect the enactments of the political branches of government and therefore the courts ought to be very cautious in holding any legislative or executive act unconstitutional. A statute should be given the presumption of constitutionality and any doubts ought to be resolved in the legislation's favour. Secondly, the judiciary should have a keen sense of its limitations. Judges should not encourage the view that the courts will be able to provide a solution to every abuse of power. The role of the judicial process is to provide a solution only if there is a legal solution available. Consequently and inevitably there will be a range of matters over which the courts cannot provide a remedy regardless of how worthy the cause is or how mischievous a legislature may have been. In those circumstances the judiciary must restrain itself from the temptation of righting every wrong. Instead the judiciary must encourage the electorate to turn to the political branches of government, and away from the courts, for redress, because that is where public policy, with a few exceptions, ought to be resolved. Above all, judicial self-restraint counsels caution in the exercise of the judicial power; it is an enormous power and ought to be used sparingly.

The difficulty with judicial self-restraint, either as an explanation or as prescriptive advice, is its imprecision. Stone's opinion in *Butler* is frequently cited as a forceful statement of the principles of self-restraint,[56] but there is a revealing episode in Joseph Lash's introductory essay to the diaries of Felix Frankfurter. The episode concerned the first of the Flag Salute cases, *Minersville School District* v. *Gobitis*.' Mr Justice Frankfurter was given the assignment to write the opinion of the Court that would sustain the authority of the state government to require a compulsory flag salute in state schools, despite the religious objections of some of the children's parents.

> There was one dissenter in the *Gobitis* case, Associate Justice Stone. When he had indicated in conference that he would dissent an agitated Frankfurter had sent him a five-page letter of his dismay. He had only been following Stone's own admonitions about judicial self-restraint, he protested. But Stone was not swayed. 'I am truly sorry not to go along with you . . .'. So strongly did Stone feel that he departed from practice to read his dissent in open Court. 'History teaches us,' he said, 'that there have been but few infringements of

personal liberty by the state which have not been justified . . . in the name of righteousness . . . and few which have not been directed . . . at helpless minorities . . .'. As for the advice of restraint, 'This seems no less than the surrender of the constitutional protection of the liberty of small minorities to the popular will'.[58]

Thus one man's self-restraint in *Butler* was the same man's unwillingness to see 'the surrender of constitutional protection' in *Gobitis*. The point about the episode is not to raise doubts over Stone's attachment to the doctrine of judicial self-restraint but merely to illustrate the difficulty of giving effect to it. Self-restraint, as Sutherland pointed out, lay 'in the domain of will not judgement'[59] and it was Stone's judgement, not will, that convinced him that restraint was the appropriate posture in *Butler* but not in *Gobitis*. For Stone, an act of will to restrain himself in *Gobitis* and accept the majority's self-restraint when he believed that a serious constitutional protection was in jeopardy, would have been misplaced. Roberts, in *Butler*, felt much the same way as Stone in *Gobitis*. Nevertheless despite the difficulties apparent with judicial self-restraint, it does have some utility as an explanatory tool. One can detect a difference between the judges on the Supreme Court between 1934 and 1936. Brandeis, Cardozo and Stone in particular were more predisposed to accept legislative utterances at face value. In *United States* v. *Constantine*, Cardozo chastised all but Brandeis and Stone for resting their judgement. 'upon the ruling that another purpose, not professed, may be read beneath the surface, and by the purpose so imputed the statute is destroyed. Thus the process of psychoanalysis has spread to unaccustomed fields.'[60] Cardozo's remark possibly over-emphasised the differences between the two sides but certainly the majority in *Constantine* and *Butler* were more zealous in their examination of legislation. In *Butler* they required a degree of proof, which a congressional declaration could not provide, that the processing tax was a revenue measure. When this further authentication was not available, the majority in *Butler* found that the processing tax was not a revenue measure. This was the reason why Roberts and Stone disagreed. There was a difference in the manner in which they evaluated legislative intention and this difference can be ascribed to Stone's greater self-restraint or to Roberts' lesser attachment to the idea.

Despite the inadequacies inherent in the notion of self-restraint, it does provide a satisfactory answer to the disagreement in *Butler*. But how does the difference between majority and minority in *Butler* over self-restraint affect the general proposition that the Court between 1934 and 1936 divided on the basis of political or social ideology and not on legal or constitutional grounds?

It must be emphasised that there was no argument in *Butler* over constitutional interpretation. There was no dispute between majority and minority over the law. They adopted the same interpretation of taxing power and the same limitation imposed by the general welfare clause. Both Stone and Roberts had the same view of the federal government's ability to regulate agricultural production. There was disagreement between them over the determination of fact which derived from a difference over an aspect of the judicial function. It was a slight but important difference which could and indeed did affect their respective decisions in certain cases where the issues were finely drawn and the legislature's intent was less than pellucid; but it is a difference which cannot be located on a spectrum of political or social ideology. Judges have been accused and indeed have accused one another of a lack of restraint for a long time. Undoubtedly the frequency of the charges was a consequence of the very imprecision of the idea of self-restraint. But the accusation came from 'liberals' against 'conservatives' and vice versa, and indeed was levelled between 'liberals' and 'conservatives'. Mr Justice Waite, a 'conservative', was a believer in restraint, whereas Mr Justice Field, also a 'conservative', could never be seen as an apostle of restraint.[61] Mr Justices Frankfurter and Douglas both sympathised with the politics of the New Deal, but while Frankfurter was the leading exponent of restraint on the Court in recent decades, Douglas could not be described in similar terms.[62] There are too many instances to be listed here of so-called 'liberal' and 'conservative' judges who shared the idea of self-restraint. The belief in judicial self-restraint reflects a vague, imprecise, but nevertheless reasonably distinct attitude to the judicial function; it does not reflect an attitude to politics or a preference for a particular set of social arrangements.

II

After *Butler* the Supreme Court on 6 April 1936 had examined the workings of the Securities and Exchange Commission but disposed of the questions raised in that case on procedural grounds.[63] On 18 May 1936, however, the Court returned to the issue that had dominated its docket for the previous sixty years, the constitutionality of a governmental economic regulation. The case of *Carter* v. *Carter Coal Co.*[64] concerned the constitutionality of the Bituminous Coal Conservation Act of 1935[65] which was intended 'to stabilize the bituminous coal-mining industry and to promote its interstate commerce'.[66] In order to give effect to this intention, Section 2 of the Act established a Bituminous Coal Commission which was authorised, with the agreement of the coal mine owners, to draw up a code for the industry.[67] Section 3 imposed an excise tax of 15 per cent on all coal mined but the levy was returned to those owners who agreed to abide by the code.[68] Section 4 directed the Commission to include provision, within the code, for minimum prices of coal products and the procedures for establishing such prices.[69] Part III Section 4 referred to the labour provisions of the code. These provisions included the right of employees in the industry to organise and bargain collectively. This right was to be protected by the creation of a board which could investigate and adjudicate any claim that employers, within the industry, were denying their employees the opportunity to organise and bargain collectively.[70] Part II of Section 4 dealt with working conditions in the industry and in particular with the maximum hour and minimum wage regulations to be incorporated in the code.[71] A stockholder in the Carter Coal Co., James W. Carter, on behalf of himself and other stockholders, sought to enjoin the company from accepting the code, from complying with its provisions and from paying the excise tax. A separate suit was filed against the collector of internal revenue to enjoin him from collecting or attempting to collect the taxes authorised under the Act. These suits arrived at the Supreme Court on writs of certiorari.

The opinion of the Court was written by Mr Justice Sutherland and supported by four of his brethren, Justices Butler, McReynolds, Roberts and Van Devanter. Chief Justice Hughes filed an opinion concurring and dissenting in part, and Justice Cardozo penned a dissent which was supported by Justices Brandeis and Stone. Predictably, Sutherland's majority opinion has not drawn, even with the passage of time, a great deal of approval. R. C. Cortner, in his monograph on the *National Labour Relations Board* v. *Jones & Laughlin Steel Corp.*[72] case views Sutherland's opinion as evidence of his colleagues, and his own 'determination to preserve as much as possible of a laissez faire economic order'.[73] Sutherland's biographer, J. F. Paschal, is more specific:

> It [Sutherland's opinion] . . . presented the country with the most decisive possible denial that the Constitution contained within its grants any authority for meeting the most serious of the problems facing the nation in 1936. The opinion, both in the expressions it employed and in the result it achieved struck the idea of American nationalism a blow such as it had seldom, if ever, received.[74]

Bernard Schwartz refers to Sutherland's 'respective interpretation of the commerce power' and its 'catastrophic consequences upon governmental regulation'. He also contrasts Sutherland's 'restrictive conception' of the Commerce Clause with Cardozo's dissent which betrayed a 'suppleness and flexibility' of interpretation.[75] Unfortunately these assessments of Sutherland's opinion are representative and indicative of the all-but-universal disapproval felt towards the majority opinion. These assessments are, however, misplaced, for Sutherland's opinion does not provide any evidence that his interpretation of the Commerce Clause was 'restrictive' or that he struck a blow against the 'idea of American nationalism' The *Carter* majority did not offer an interpretation of the Commerce Clause that established new restrictions or applied earlier interpretations in a newly restrictive manner. Indeed there was no disagreement between the *Carter* majority and the other four judges over the Commerce Clause aspects of the Bituminous Coal Conservation Act; their disagreements lay elsewhere and were far less substantial than commentaries on the case have suggested.

There were five questions to be resolved in *Carter*. Firstly, were the stockholders entitled to bring their suit? Secondly, if they were entitled to do so, had they brought their suit prematurely? Thirdly, were the procedures established for setting the hours and wages regulations in the coal industry an excessive delegation of legislative power and a violation of the due process clause of the Fifth Amendment? Fourthly, was the excise tax a revenue measure or a penalty for non-compliance with the code? Finally, were the price and labour regulations a legitimate exercise of congressional power under the Commerce Clause? The entire Court was in agreement that the stockholders did have a right to bring a suit and they were also agreed that the timing of the action was not premature, although Cardozo did enter a caveat over one aspect of the stockholders' claim.[76] However, there was disagreement over the procedures in the code for establishing the maximum hours and minimum wage regulations. The five justices of the majority were joined by Hughes in their belief that the procedures constituted an unlawful delegation of legislative power and also violated the due process clause of the law. The reason for their belief was that the power to frame the regulations was delegated to 'the producers of more than two-thirds of the annual tonnage production and to more than one-half of the mine workers employed'.[77] According to Sutherland, the consequence of this act of delegation

> in respect of wages is to subject the dissentient minority, either of producers or miners or both to the will of the stated majority since by refusing to submit the minority at once incurs the hazard of enforcement ... of the act ... The power conferred upon the majority is, in effect, the power to regulate the affairs of an unwilling minority. This is legislative delegation in its most obnoxious form; for it is not delegation to an official body, presumably disinterested, but to private persons whose interests may be and often are adverse to the interest of others in the same business.[78]

In Sutherland's judgement, the delegation of power was so clearly arbitrary that it was also a 'denial of rights safeguarded by the due process clause of the Fifth Amendment'.[79] Interestingly, Cardozo entirely ignored Sutherland's objections and did not take issue with him over the composition of the body that set the levels for the minimum wage and maximum hours. Instead he directed his remarks at whether the Bituminous Coal Conservation Act provided sufficient guidance to the body in its task of establishing the appropriate levels. Cardozo concluded that 'the standards established by this Act are quite as definite as others that have had the approval of this court'.[80] The difference between Cardozo and Sutherland can be ascribed to self-restraint. Where Cardozo was prepared to resolve a doubt that the procedures may be prejudicial in favour of the Act, Sutherland was unwilling to restrain his belief that the procedures were inherently prejudicial to the interests of the minority of owners and miners. However, the disagreement was not a substantial one and Sutherland's holding did not irreparably damage the Act. Indeed Sutherland himself offered a solution when he implied that the flaw could be remedied if the authority that imposed the wage and hours regulation was both 'official' and 'impartial'

The fourth question, the nature of the excise tax, also caused a division on the Court. The reference to the argument over the excise tax in *Carter* was the same as in *United States* v. *Butler* and was accepted by all nine judges. The Congress could impose an excise tax if it was a revenue measure but it could not impose a regulation masquerading as a tax on an industry which it had no authority to regulate. The majority believed that the tax was indeed a disguised regulation of activities that were not within the jurisdiction of Congress, while Cardozo, Brandeis and Stone shared the view that the tax was valid because Congress was acting within its constitutional authority. Did this imply, as the commentary on the case suggests, a substantial difference of opinion between the two sides over the extent of congressional power under the Commerce Clause? The answer is no; there was not a major disagreement on this point and this is apparent if the responses to the fifth question are examined closely.

The fifth question that the Court had to resolve was, did the Congress have the authority under the Commerce Clause to regulate both prices and labour conditions in the coal industry? Six judges, the majority plus Hughes, declared that the Congress did not possess the authority to impose the 'fair labour' practices of the code. It cannot be emphasised too strongly that Cardozo, Brandeis and Stone did not dissent from this holding, because in 1936 congressional regulation of manufacturing or production processes in general was not constitutionally permissible. Sutherland had little difficulty in demonstrating there was a line of authority which deemed manufacturing and commerce to be separate and distinguishable activities. Congress could regulate commerce but not manufacturing. In 1888 the Court offered this analysis: 'No distinction is . . . more clearly expressed in economic and political literature than that between manufacturers and commerce. Manufacture is transformation – the fashioning of raw materials into change of form for use. The functions of commerce are different. The buying and selling and the transportation incidental thereto constitute commerce.'[81] Then the Court, almost anticipating the argument which would be raised in subsequent years that manufacturing and indeed all processes of production impinged on commerce, pointed out the consequences if the power to regulate commerce incorporated the power to regulate production: 'The result would be that Congress would be invested . . . with the power to regulate, not only manufacture but also agriculture, horticulture, stock-raising . . . in short every branch of human industry. For is there one of them that does not contemplate, more or less clearly an interstate or foreign market?[82] In *United States* v. *E. C. Knight Co.*,[83] Chief Justice Fuller reaffirmed this distinction:

> Doubtless the power to control the manufacture of a given thing involves in a certain sense the control of its disposition, but this is secondary and not the primary sense; and although the exercise of that power may result in bringing the operation of commerce into play, it does not control it, and affects it only incidentally and indirectly. Commerce succeeds to manufacture and is not a part of it . . . The fact that an article is manufactured for export to another State does not of itself make it an article of interstate commerce. . .[84]

In *Oliver Iron Co.* v. *Lord*[85] the Court equated mining with manufacturing: 'Mining is not interstate commerce, but like manufacturing is a local business subject to local regulation and taxation. Its character . . . is intrinsic'.[86] Thus if mining was the equivalent of manufacturing then it too was excluded from congressional control. What authority did the Congress possess to impose labour regulations on the coal industry? Certainly when the Bituminous Coal Conservation Act was working its way through Congress there 'were strong doubts about the constitutionality of the measure' in both houses which were only finally assuaged by President Roosevelt when he declared his own belief, in a letter to a Congressman, that the Act was constitutional.[87] The doubts of Congressmen and Senators were not based on lack of congressional authority to regulate the commercial activities of the coal industry. Their hesitation derived from the established assumption at the time that the conditions of employment affected production, not commerce. Consequently unless it could be successfully argued that labour conditions within an industry affected the interstate commercial activities of that industry, then the Act would encounter constitutional obstacles. Of course it could be mooted that labour conditions almost certainly impinged on an industry's interstate commercial activities. In 1936, however, any such claim would be inevitably followed by the direct–indirect effect on interstate commerce test. Did labour relations constitute a direct or an indirect effect on that industry's interstate commercial activities? Sutherland applied such a test and his conclusion was that the effect was indirect, which was the usual result in such cases. After all, only a year earlier in *Schechter*, the Court had also held a code incorporating 'fair labour' provisions unconstitutional.

The argument that is being developed here is that in 1936, interpretation of the Commerce Clause did not permit the Congress to regulate a production or aspects of the processes of production unless there was an effect on commerce over and above the effect that production normally had on commerce. Now it is not being suggested that the interpretation of the Commerce Clause was correct or that it dealt satisfactorily with the reality of interstate commerce in 1930s. Indeed there is a very strong argument that the courts during that decade should have been reconsidering some of their doctrines in this area, including the distinction between manufacturing and commerce. Nevertheless at the time of *Carter* v. *Carter Coal Co.*, the Commerce Clause was being interpreted in such a manner. Therefore, Sutherland cannot be successfully accused of creating a new restriction on congressional power or applying an existing interpretation of the Commerce Clause with a newly devised restrictive twist. The fact that Sutherland was reiterating an established doctrine was acknowledged tacitly in Cardozo's dissent. He did not take issue with the majority opinion over the labour provisions but directed his attention to the price regulations. Both Cardozo and Hughes focused their discussions of the Commerce Clause with reference to the price regulations, which they found to be within the power of the Congress. Cardozo and Hughes were able, with considerable ease, to demonstrate that prices or charges had always been deemed to be an appropriate subject for the exercise of commerce power. Sutherland *et al.* did not dissent from this assessment. The power of Congress to regulate prices of products in interstate commerce was too well established. The point of dissension between the sides was whether the price and labour provisions could be considered separately. If they could, as Cardozo and Hughes argued, the price regulations would be constitutional but the labour provisions would be held invalid. But according to the majority opinion the two regulations were not 'like a collection of bricks, some of which may be taken away without disturbing the others, but rather are like the interwoven threads constituting the warp and woof of a fabric, one set of which cannot be removed without fatal consequences to the whole'.[88] This difference over statutory construction was significant as far as the settlement of the litigation was concerned, but it is not important to the discussion here. What is important here is that the nine judges were in agreement on the broad issues of constitutional interpretation. Sutherland had not withdrawn from the judicial consensus that Congress could regulate the prices of goods and services in interstate commerce. The Congress was able, post-*Carter*, to incorporate the price provisions of the Bituminous Coal Conservation Act in a new statute. Thus there was no judicial dispute over the Commerce Clause in *Carter*. The two sides were in agreement on both the labour and price regulations because they shared the same broad interpretation of the Clause.

*Carter* was the last case concerning important federal regulation to come before the Court until 1937.[89] But in 1937 Van Devanter resigned and indeed by 1941 only two judges remained – Roberts, and Stone who became Chief Justice. President Roosevelt who had not made one appointment to the Supreme Court between 1933 and 1937 was able to make seven appointments in the following four years.[90] So in a sense *Carter* marked the end of a chapter in the Court's history. Between 1934 and 1936 the Court did have a distinctive response to the New Deal, but that response had drawn an all-but-universal censure. G. Edward White reflects this hostility: 'The actions of the Court in the 1930s appeared so transparently political, and the reasoning of many decisions so tortured that critics began to ask whether any stature remained in the judicial branch of government.'[91]

It has been argued here that the Court's response to the New Deal cases between 1934 and 1936 plus *Blaisdell* and *Nebbia* was not, as White and countless others have suggested, politically motivated. The contention is that judges did not cast their vote in these cases because of their own personal predilection for a particular set of economic and social arrangements. Consequently there was no great division among the so-called 'liberal three', the 'four horsemen of reaction' and the two 'swingmen' A more adequate and convincing answer to the pattern and structure of judicial decisions lies in the nature of the legal process – an argument which will now be more fully developed.

## NOTES

1 On 9 December 1935, the Supreme Court unanimously declared sections of the Home Owners Loan Act of 1933, as amended in 1934 and 1935, unconstitutional. Mr Justice Cardozo wrote the opinion and found these sections of the Act in violation of the Tenth Amendment. See *Hopkins Federal Savings and Load Association* v. *Cleary et al.*, 296 US 315 (1935).

2 'Constitutional Revolution' is a phrase coined by Edward Corwin to describe what others have referred to as the 'switch in time that saved nine', i.e. the 'change' that took place on the Court after President Roosevelt's 'court-packing' proposals. See E. Corwin, *Constitutional Revolution Ltd.* (1941), pp.64, 65.

3 48 Stat. 31.

4 49 Stat. 991.

5 297 US 1 (1936).

6 298 US 238 (1936).

7 298 US 587 (1936).

8 L. Baker, *Back to Back: The Duel Between FDR and the Supreme Court* (1967), pp. 117–46.

9 See J. Schideler, *Farm Crisis, 1919–1923* (1957), *passim*.

10 R. Tugwell, *The Battle for Democracy* (1935), p. 109.

11 Senator Charles L. McNary of Oregon and Representative Gilbert N. Haugen of Iowa agreed to introduce in Congress proposals which had been devised by George N. Peek and Hugh S. Johnson of the Moline Plow Company.

12 G. Fite, *George N. Peek and the Fight for Farm Parity* (1954), p. 60.

13 *Ibid.*, p. 61.

14 V. Perkins, *Crisis in Agriculture* (1969), pp. 23, 24.

15 W. Rowley, *M. L. Wilson and the Campaign for Domestic Allotment* (1970), pp. 142–77.

16 The one exception was the Farmers' Union. C. Campbell, *The Farm Bureau and the New Deal* (1962), p. 55.

17 The list of commodities mentioned is not complete; there were other commodities such as logs, milk products and peanuts. But clearly wheat and cotton were the most important crops to be regulated.

18 The parity price for tobacco was August 1919 – July 1929. See the Agricultural Adjustment Act, Title I, Section 2.

19 Agricultural Adjustment Act, Title I, Section 8.

20 *Ibid.*, Section 9.

21 *Ibid.*, Section 8, Clause 2.

22 *Ibid.*, p. Section 8, Clause 3.

23 Perkins, *Crisis in Agriculture*, note 14, pp. 47, 48.

24 *Newsweek*, 21 December 1935, p. 30.

25 297 US 1, 44 (1936).

26 A. Schlesinger Jr, *The Politics of Upheaval* (1966), p. 471.

27 262 US 447 (1923).

28 *Ibid.*, p. 488.

29 *Ibid.*, p. 487.

30 *Brief for the United States, United States* v. *Butler et al*, p. 137.

31 297 US 1, 65 (1936).

32 J. Story, *Commentaries on the Constitutions of the United States* (1883). For an intelligent discussion of Story's constitutional doctrine see, J. McClellan, *Joseph Storey and the American Constitution* (1971).

33 297 US 1, 66 (1936).

34 By 1933 the federal government had appropriated money on a number of occasions to aid aspects of the agricultural industry. In 1884 the Bureau of Animal Husbandry was established to disseminate information as to domestic animals and their diseases. In 1916, the Federal Farm Loan Act provided a rural credit system. In 1929, Congress established the Federal Farm Board to promote the effective merchandising of agricultural commodities.

35 297 US 1, 58, 59 (1936).

36 *Ibid.*, p. 59.

37 *Ibid.*, p. 73.

38 'Congress', wrote Chief Justice Marshall 'is not empowered to tax for those purposes which are within the exclusive power of the States.' *Gibbons* v. *Ogden*, 9 Wheat. 1, 199 (1824).

39 259 US 16 (1922). For an extended discussion of the Child Labor Tax Case see, S. Wood, *Constitutional Politics in the Progressive Era: Child Labor and the Law* (1968), pp. 255–99.

40 *Ibid.*, p. 67.

41 *Hill* v. *Wallace*, 259 US 44 (1922).

42 296 US 287 (1935).

43 *Ibid.*, p. 296.

44 297 US 1, 68 (1936).

45 Mr Justice Roberts noticed the government's omission to suggest that the Act could be sustained on grounds other than the taxing power. In particular he appeared surprised that the government had not suggested the Commerce Clause as a source of congressional authority. 'The Government does not attempt to uphold the validity of the Act on the basis of the commerce clause, which, for the purpose of the present case, may be put aside as irrelevant.' 297 US 1, 64 (1936).

46 *Ibid.*, pp. 70, 71.

47 *Ibid.*, p. 85.

**48** For instance see the Morrill Land Grant Act.
**49** 297 US 1, 79, 80 (1936).
**50** *Ibid.*, pp. 78, 79.
**51** 6 Cranch. 87 (1910).
**52** *Munn* v. *Illinois*, 94 US 113, 123 (1877).
**53** *Ibid.*, p. 134.
**54** 369 US 186 (1962).
**55** *Ibid.*, p. 270.
**56** See S. Konefsky, *Chief Justice Stone and the Supreme Court* (1946), pp. 116, 117.
**57** 310 US 586 (1940). The other Flag Salute case was *West Virginia State Board of Education* v. *Barnette*, 319 US 624 (1943) where the *Gobitis* rule was reversed.
**58** J. Lash, *From the Diaries of Felix Frankfurter* (1975), p. 69.
**59** *West Coast Hotel* v. *Parrish*, 300 US 379, 402 (1937).
**60** 296 US 287, 298, 299 (1935).
**61** *Munn* v. *Illinois*, 94 US 113 (1876) is a good example of Waite's judicial style as is Field's dissent in that case. See also his opinion in the Slaughter-House Cases, 16 Wall. 36 (1873). Robert McCloskey demonstrates Field's lack of attachment to self-restraint in his book on American conservatism. See R. G. McCloskey, *American Conservatism in the Age of Enterprise* (1951), pp. 72–104.
**62** Frankfurter's commitment to restraint is documented in W. Mendelson, *Justices Black and Frankfurter: Conflict in the Court* (1966).
**63** *Jones* v. *Securities Exchange Commission*, 298 US 1 (1936).
**64** 298 US 238 (1936).
**65** The Bituminous Coal Conservation Act was also known as the Guffey-Snyder Act after its sponsors Senator Joseph Guffey and Representative J. Buell Snyder, both of Pennsylvania.
**66** 298 US 238, 279 (1936).
**67** *Ibid.*, p. 280.
**68** *Ibid.*, pp. 280, 281.
**69** *Ibid.*, pp. 281, 282.
**70** *Ibid.*, pp. 283, 284.
**71** *Ibid.*, p. 282.
**72** 301 US 1 (1937).
**73** R. C. Cortner, *The Jones & Laughlin Case* (1970), p. 106.
**74** J. Paschal, *Mr Justice Sutherland: A Man Against the State* (1951), p. 198.
**75** B. Schwartz, *A Commentary on the Constitution of the United States: The Powers of Government*, Vol. I (1963), pp. 187, 194.
**76** Cardozo argued that the 'suits are premature in so far as they seek a judicial declaration as to the validity or invalidity of the regulations in respect of labour embodied in Part III'. 295 US 238, 324 (1936).
**77** *Ibid.*, p. 310.
**78** *Ibid.*, p. 311.
**79** *Ibid.*, p. 311.
**80** *Ibid.*, p. 333.
**81** *Kidd* v. *Pearson*, 128 US 1, 20 (1888).
**82** *Ibid.*, p. 21.
**83** 156 US 1 (1895).
**84** *Ibid.*, pp. 12, 13.
**85** 262 US 172 (1923).
**86** *Ibid.*, p. 178.
**87** E. Hawley, *The New Deal and the Problem of Monopoly* (1966), p. 207.
**88** 298 US 238, 315, 316 (1936).
**89** In *Ashton* v. *Cameron County Dist.*, 298 US 513 (1936), the Court held the

Municipal Bankruptcy Act of 1934 unconstitutional on Tenth Amendment grounds. It has not been examined as it does not materially affect the discussion.

90 Justice Van Devanter resigned in June 1937, and was followed by Sutherland in January 1938. They were replaced by Justices Black and Reed respectively. Cardozo died in 1938 and was replaced by Felix Frankfurter and the replacements for Brandeis, Butler and Hughes were Justices Douglas, Murphy and Jackson (who in fact replaced Stone after his appointment to Chief Justice).

91 G. E. White, *The American Judicial Tradition* (1976), pp. 197, 198.

# 7

# Conclusion

I would like to return to some of the broader considerations raised in Chapter 1 over the nature of judicial process. Clearly those considerations can only be discussed within the context of the the decisions that have been examined. Nevertheless there are some important and interesting observations that can be made.

In each of the cases examined, there was at least one claim that the legislation concerned was constitutionally flawed. In each case the Court did not have to return to the Constitution, it did not have to resort to a textual analysis of that document. It did not have to do so because the questions raised in these cases were not virgin issues. The Commerce Clause and due process questions, in particular, had dominated the business of the Court in the preceding decades. Consequently by the 1930s, the Supreme Court was evaluating due process and Commerce Clause claims within an established inter-pretation of these sections. In other words it was guided and limited by the rules enunciated by the Court in previous years. Even in those cases like *Blaisdell* where there was an extended discussion of constitutional intent in relation to the Contract Clause, the Court's reference was set by the rules in *Bronson* v. *Kinzie*, *Howard* v. *Bugbee*, *Block* v. *Hirsh*, etc. The Court in *Blaisdell* and in the other cases was evaluating the constitutionality of legislation within a reference of legal rules that had been developed over the years. However, even if this point is accepted, that judicial decisions are made within a reference constructed by legal rules, it must be conceded that the reference is sufficiently imprecise to permit disagreement between judges. The Court, after all, was only in full agreement over *Schechter* and *Radford* and all but unanimous in *Panama Refining Co.* It was divided, however, over *Butler* and *Carter* and the decisions in the Gold Clause cases, *Railroad Retirement Board, Nebbia* and

*Blaisdell* were sustained by a majority of one vote. Consequently the claim is made that if legal rules do not provide judges with an unambiguous answer to the question posed in the litigation, then it is entirely feasible that judges make a decision based on their personal policy preferences and then search for an appropriate rule to provide their policy predilection with a legal rationale. After all, say the behaviouralists and the rule-sceptics, there are rules available to sustain a variety of judicial options so a judge has little difficulty in obtaining a cloak of legal and judicial respectability. It is an argument which has, if not the ring of truth, the ring of feasibility, but whether it can withstand a closer examination is another matter.

The above argument is based on two propositions. The first is that legal rules in appellate cases do not provide judges with an explicit and unambiguous answer to the problems raised in the litigation, and secondly if legal rules do not offer a definitive answer, judges can ignore them and make decisions based on other considerations and use the rules as a *post hoc* justification.[1] The first proposition is essentially correct and is offered in response to the inflated claim for legal rules in a Blackstonian jurisprudence. The notion that a judge merely applies the 'appropriate' rule to the facts under consideration is not a convincing portrait of the judicial function at the appellate court level. It claims too much for the role of legal rules and too little for the enormously difficult task of adjudication. It is a view that is hard to sustain post-Holmes and Cardozo. Even in those legal systems, such as England, where the doctrine of *stare decisis* holds, and the judiciary are obliged to apply the authoritative rule, there is disagreement between judges over which rule is authoritative. Judges in England are not mechanical dispensers of precedent. Consequently in the United States, where *stare decisis* has never achieved quite the same authority as in England, a 'slot-machine' theory of jurisprudence is certainly no longer acceptable. It has been apparent for a considerable period of time that the judicial function incorporates an element of creativity. But having disposed of the idea that legal rules provide judges with unambiguous answers, the second proposition proceeds to assume that rules offer judges no guidance and no answers. This is a much more tendentious proposition for it does not necessarily follow that because the rigid formalism of Blackstone is inadequate, it must be replaced by a version of the legal process lacking any formal structure. If a view that judges do not exercise any discretion because the rules do not permit them discretion is invalid, it does not mean that judges have an unlimited discretion which includes the option to impose judicial solutions based on their own political and social desires. Furthermore, a reluctance in America to endow the doctrine of stare decisis with the authority it has in England does not mean the American judiciary are ready or willing to dispose with the decisions of the past.

> To follow past decisions is natural and indeed a necessary procedure . . . To take the same course as has been taken previously, or has usually been adopted in the past, not only confers the advantage of the accumulated experience of the past but also saves the effort of having to think out a problem anew each time it arises . . . Precedent has thus always been the life-blood of legal systems, whether primitive, archaic or modern.[2]

Thus judges cannot afford to ignore previous decisions for if they did, every settled argument would be reopened. Every litigant would have his day in court plus a further day and another day after that; there would be no end in sight. The legal process would be drained of that vital attribute of certainty which gives it authority. Precedent obviously does play a vital role in judicial decision-making which cannot be denied. What can be denied is that legal rules provide unambiguous solutions in all cases. For there is a category of appellate cases where the existing rules are unclear, unsatisfactory or inadequate and it is the task of the judge to clarify the rule or replace it. This task requires judicial creativity but the creativity is guided by mutually agreed notions of reasoning and argument. This is an intermediate position between those who argue that judges have no discretion and others who declare that judicial discretion is absolute. It is a position which denies the rigid formalism of Blackstone and the subjectivist anarchy of judicial behaviouralism.

What are the processes of reasoning that offer guidance and instruction to a judge in the task of adjudication? Perhaps they can be discerned from those cases that were discussed and where the governing rule was less than satisfactory or in need of clarification. In *Blaisdell* the Court faced a position where the rule governing the abridgement of contract by state legislatures was unclear, and in *Nebbia* the majority on the Court believed that the controlling doctrine of an 'industry affected with the public interest' was unsatisfactory. Both these cases illustrate the potential for creativity that resides within the judicial function and the limitations within which that creativity functions. If *Blaisdell* is taken first, the rule governing the abridgement of contract had been most explicitly enunciated in *Bronson* v. *Kinzie*[3] that the Contract Clause did not permit a direct as opposed to an incidental abridgement of contract. This rule had been reasserted on several occasions since 1843 but the clarity of the rule had been muddled by the Rent Cases,[4] where the Court had permitted a contract to be directly abridged but without an extended discussion of Contract Clause protections. Consequently the alternatives that faced the Court in *Blaisdell* was firstly a reassertion of *Bronson* and the dismissal of the Rent Cases as an aberration, a position which was adopted by the minority. Secondly the Court could have confirmed the implicit assumptions of the Rent Cases, or thirdly it could have provided a new rule which was the route the majority opinion of Chief Justice Hughes chose to follow. The rule that Hughes created allowed a state legislature to abridge a contract directly, but only in an emergency and under careful judicial supervision, which would provide an assurance that no fundamental property rights were being abused. In other words Hughes attempted to encompass the protections of *Bronson* and the flexibility of the Rent Cases in the same rule. It was a solution which illustrates both the limitations and creativity of the judicial function. The essential protections of the Contract Clause were left untouched but at the same time the new rule offered the state legislatures an extra weapon in their arsenal to cope with the consequences of the economic depression. It was an attempt by the Court to adapt the *Bronson* rule to the economic realities of the 1930s but in a manner which would not seriously reduce the protections offered by *Bronson*. How did Hughes justify the creation of the new rule? The central element in the rule was the notion of emergency powers. In an emergency a state legislature had the power to abridge contracts but when the emergency passed so did the legislature's authority to intervene in private contractual obligations. The process of justification of this grant of emergency powers to the state legislatures resulted from Hughes' use of analogical reasoning or what Edward Levi calls 'reasoning by example'.[5] The example that Hughes used was the war powers of the President which are also normally dormant but come into operation in a particular and defined set of circumstances. The war powers of the President provided an apt analogy for emergency powers in *Blaisdell* and it meant that Hughes was not introducing a new doctrine but merely applying an existing doctrine to a different series of circumstances: an activity which is central to the processes of legal argument. The use of analogical reasoning is both a principal characteristic of legal argument and a limitation on judicial creativity. When a judge is modifying an existing rule or creating a new one it is incumbent on him to demonstrate by analogy that the new rule conforms with extant doctrines. Hughes was able to achieve this in *Blaisdell*. The doctrine of emergency powers was not new, nor did he seriously reduce the protections of the Contract Clause; nevertheless he did give the state legislatures a further option in their attempt to provide their citizens with a measure of economic relief. The *Blaisdell* rule is an example of creativity but a creativity exercised within limits. It is not an instance where a judge made a rule on the basis of his preferences but an example where a judge, using the greatest delicacy and weaving a sophisticated argument, attempted to achieve a fine balance between the exercise of legislative power and the constitutional restrictions.

The case of *Nebbia* v. *New York* raised problems of a different ilk to *Blaisdell*. The governing rule was perfectly clear but the question was, had it outlived its usefulness? From the Court's perspective in 1934 the governing rule to be applied to the facts in *Nebbia* was clear. State legislatures could only regulate the prices of those industries which were 'affected with the public interest'. This rule had been formulated in the 1877 case of *Munn* v. *Illinois*[6] and it is clear from the text of Chief Justice Waite's opinion in *Munn* that he believed a large number of industries were so affected. However, the 'affected with the public interest' rule was so imprecise that the courts were obliged to adopt a more meaningful standard to distinguish between industries which were not 'affected with the public interest' from those that were. In the search for these standards and from an understandable desire for greater precision and certainty, the courts reduced the list of industries that fell within the 'affected with the public interest' category, so that by 1934 'affected with the public interest' had become synonymous with public utility. Paradoxically this meant that state governments pre-*Munn* had more authority to legislate over these matters than did the state government in the 1920s and 1930s. Before 1877 government regulations of the economy were evaluated within the context of the due process clause of the Fourteenth Amendment and the reasonable exercise of the police power, and this formulation offered both protection against an arbitrary use of power and a greater latitude to the state legislature in dealing with economic problems than was available to state legislatures under the restricted *Munn* doctrine of *Chas. Wolff Packing Co.* v. *Industrial Court*[7] and *Ribnik* v. *McBride*.[8] The majority of the Court in *Nebbia* believed that this was an untenable position because the grave circumstances facing the State of New York required that the government there should have the same range of powers that state governments possessed pre-1877. The *Nebbia* majority were able to achieve this by framing a rule that essentially restored the pre-*Munn* position, by returning the evaluation of constitutionality to a consideration of due process and police power issues and dispensing with the 'affected with the public interest' doctrine, and this new rule offered a very real protection against the abuse of property rights. The *Nebbia* decision is therefore an example of judicial adaptation to the economic realities of the moment but through a cautious development of extant rules and principles. The Court was able in *Nebbia* to provide the government of New York with a more flexible response to the economic depression, but was able to do so without a decisive break with the past. Indeed Mr Justice Roberts' opinion used the earlier decisions of the Court creatively and intelligently in an attempt to restore the historically desired but delicate balance between property rights and governmental power, which Roberts believed had been upset by the restrictive development of the *Munn* doctrine. *Nebbia* like *Blaisdell* is an example of judicial discretion in operation but a discretion that is both guided and limited.

138

There are two questions that immediately arise from this analysis of *Nebbia* and *Blaisdell*. If these two cases were examples of judicial adaptation, albeit cautious and incremental adaptation, to the economic realities of the 1930s, why was the Court less accommodating for instance in *Schechter* and *Carter*? Secondly, why were the dissenting judges in *Nebbia* and *Blaisdell* unwilling to accede to the process of judicial accommodation to the changing economic and social milieu? If the question of the Court's response in *Schechter* and *Butler* is taken first, it has been argued above that there was no substantial disagreement on the Court over Commerce Clause interpretation. The nine judges were agreed about what constituted commerce and they all accepted the distinctions that had been developed between intrastate and interstate, and between the direct and indirect effect on interstate commerce. However, it is open to question how useful these definitions and distinctions were. It could be argued, particularly with hindsight, that the distinction between interstate and intrastate and the direct/indirect formula were less than valuable tools in decision-making because the governing interdependence of the American economy made it difficult to apply these distinctions. After all, these rules had been developed in a period when the line between interstate and intrastate could be clearly drawn, but by the 1930s the line could not be drawn so easily. The live poultry industry was perhaps an example of local industry, but it was one of a dwindling number of such industries. The line between interstate and intrastate industries was increasingly difficult to draw and there were also fewer and fewer industries on the intrastate side of the line. Consequently, it was a rule that was coming to the end of its judicial usefulness and the judiciary would have to re-evaluate it. Why did they not do so in *Schechter* and *Carter* and also take the opportunity to re-examine the direct/indirect rule which was also becoming untenable? The principal reason why the Court did not take the opportunity in *Schechter* and *Carter* to revise these rules is that the judicial process, at least in the 1930s, responded both slowly and incrementally. The claim for federal governmental authority that was made in the National Industrial Recovery Act and the Bituminous Coal Conservation Act constituted a sharp break with the past. In the National Industrial Recovery Act for instance, the federal government claimed the power to regulate most aspects of virtually every industry. If the Court had accepted the claim in *Schechter* it would have meant the immediate overruling of the existing governing rules, but more than that, it would have required the abandonment forthwith of the central organising concept of Commerce Clause interpretation, up to that point in time, that there was a limitation to the powers of the federal government over commerce and that the role of the judiciary was to establish the precise boundaries of this limitation. It was therefore feasible for the Court to discard the direct/indirect dichotomy or the interstate/intrastate distinction in its search for a more suitable rule, but it was entirely another matter for it to say that the Commerce Clause imposed no restrictions on the powers of the federal government. It was certainly most unlikely to do so in 1934 for even if the Court should finally adopt the position that the Commerce Clause did not restrict the federal government, it was only going to do so with considerable deliberation. The Court would require both time, and evidence that the existing rules were inadequate and no longer appropriate for the facts and that there was no possibility of fashioning other judicial doctrines which were able to cope with the new economic realities. If the Supreme Court had been convinced that this was the position, there could well have been a different response in *Schechter* and *Carter* on the Commerce Clause questions. The process of judicial adaptation is slow; the courts require time and rules change but they do so gradually. The Roosevelt administration simply expected far too much from the courts. The New Dealers expected the judiciary to be sympathetic to their belief that the times demanded innovative and drastic remedies. But the nature of the judicial function, at least as it was perceived in the 1930s, did not permit the judiciary to change direction sharply. Politicians could do so but not judges. Consequently the New Deal's difficulties with the Court did not result from the political preferences and attitudes of the judges but arose because judges were responding in a judicially proper manner to legislation which claimed significant new powers for the federal government.

The response of all nine judges, however, was not uniform. If *Blaisdell* and *Nebbia* are examples of a gradual judicial accommodation to the economic facts of the 1930s, why did four judges dissent in both cases? The answer possibly provides the key to the disagreements on the Court in the economic regulation cases between 1934 and 1936. There is no doubt, if the dissenting opinions in *Blaisdell* and *Nebbia* are examined, that Sutherland and McReynolds respectively were less aware of the creative possibilities residing within the judicial function than either Hughes or Roberts. Where the quality of the argument employed by Hughes in *Blaisdell* is light and dexterous, Sutherland's opinion by contrast is heavy and plodding. In *Blaisdell*, Sutherland betrays an unfortunate tendency to close doors prematurely and to suggest that issues have been decided definitively so that they can be locked away, never to be re-examined. Hughes' argument in *Blaisdell* is a sophisticated and delicate construction, whereas no such 'accusation' can be levelled at Sutherland's opinion. There was a certain vulgarity and crudeness about the judicial mind of Sutherland and this was true of McReynolds.[9] They did not have an eye for detail or a sense of nuance. They did not search for the shades of difference between cases which enables the creativity of a judge to come into operation. To put it bluntly, they were not very good judges. They did not possess the qualities of Hughes, Cardozo or even Roberts. They did not have the subtlety of mind to recognise that the decisions in *Blaisdell* and *Nebbia* were not reducing the constitutional protections offered to property rights. The charge is often made that Sutherland and McReynolds should not have sat on the Court because of their political biases, which is both unfair and inaccurate; it could be said, however, that they should not have been on the Court because they were not very good judges. When Sutherland wrote in *West Coast Hotel* v. *Parrish*[10] that 'self-restraint belongs in the domain of will and not judgement', he was essentially correct. There was no problem over Sutherland's control of his will, but there is a problem with the quality of his and McReynolds' judgement. This is a point that is rarely made because there is an unfortunate inclination among some students of the legal process to see disagreements between judges over constitutional interpretation, a reflection of disagreements over matters such as policy, politics or social ideology. There is no room in such a conception to explain disagreements in terms of the relative abilities of judges.

This is misguided because between 1934 and 1936 there *were* differences in ability between the nine judges and these differences *did* have significant consequences. The more acute and intelligent judges were able to use the judicial process more creatively and they did attempt to provide a greater degree of judicial accommodation to the changing nature of the American economy. Of course, they carried this task out cautiously and within the mutually-agreed actions of the judicial process and by using shared modes of argument and reasoning. But it was a task which the less subtle and sophisticated judges found difficult to appreciate, let alone emulate, a point which must be emphasised. Because if, for example, Sutherland's and Hughes' opinions in Blaisdell are seen only as manifestations of different political traditions, they are treated as political documents rather than judicial texts, which works to the detriment of Hughes' opinion. Hughes' opinion is a judicial *tour de force*, it is skilfully and finely crafted, but when it is examined for its political doctrines it is no better or worse than Sutherland's stolid opinion. Consequently, to consider judicial opinion as anything other than judicial texts is to deny, or at best, to ignore the craft of a judge and to relegate judicial craftsmanship and professional skill into insignificance. But craftsmanship in judges is as significant as it is in any other professional activity, and in any other professional activity the quality of craftsmanship is an important criterion for distinguishing between individual practitioners. It is no less important a criterion for distinguishing between judges on the United States Supreme Court and it does offer a useful tool in explaining the differences that existed on the Court between 1934 and 1936, particularly if it is used in conjunction with the differences over self-restraint that was evident in *Butler*.

If this chapter has concentrated primarily on the apparent inconsistencies of decisions and the differences between judges, the book as a whole has argued that the judges on the United States Supreme Court between 1934 and 1936 were fundamentally in agreement. They agreed over the broad issues of constitutional interpretation and over the essential nature of the judicial function. They had a common view of the process for evaluating the constitutionality of legislation and used mutually-agreed modes of reasoning and argument in carrying out this evaluation. In the cases examined, all nine judges perceived the same questions even if they differed over the answers. They perceived the same problems because they all recognised the importance of legal rules, which set the context for the exercise of the judicial discretion. Extant rules set the reference and defined the issues in the litigation that came before them. Legal rules were consequently a crucial factor in judicial decision-making. Of course this does not mean that the rules were entirely determinative because they were not, but they set the reference within which judicial discretion was exercised. Within the reference set by the rules, judges did offer differing responses to the questions raised in the cases, but these differences can perhaps be accounted for by the variations in ability and skill among the nine judges and by their attachment to such notions as self-restraint. Consequently the central argument is that the Supreme Court's decisions in the economic regulation cases of those two years can only be understood within a judicial and legal context. The realist version of judicial decision-making ignores the particular characteristics of the judicial and legal process. It treats judicial decision-making as just another variant of political decision-making. In doing so, most realists discard all that is unique in judicial decision-making. No-one can deny the impact of the decisions made by the United States Supreme Court on the American polity, but it is vital to distinguish political impact from the process of decision-making. The impact is political but the decision-making process is legal and judicial.

To conclude, this book has argued that legal rules set the reference for judicial decision-making in the economic regulation cases that came before the Supreme Court between 1934 and 1936. It has suggested that these rules offered the judges guidance and direction and was a critically important factor in judicial decision-making. It has offered the text of the judicial opinions as evidence of this proposition and it is clear from these texts, if they can be trusted, that the decisions were affected by the rules. But why is it not possible that judges were merely paying lip service to the importance of earlier decisions and in fact were more concerned with their personal policy predilections? There are two different responses to this question. The first is that the art of dissembling is a profoundly difficult one, particularly if it is to be carried out by all judges in every opinion. It would be most unlikely that a close textual analysis of an opinion would not reveal any indications of this judicial sleight of hand. Moreover, it would have required a degree of dishonesty which is simply inconceivable of the Chief Justice or Van Devanter or indeed any of the others. The second response would be to answer the question with a question. Why would judges bother to disguise their desire to make policy? Presumably only because policy-making was deemed to be an improper activity for a judge. But if it was an activity that was frowned on, why should judges wish to behave improperly? There is no reason why judges as a category would want to violate their professional beliefs, and that is the point; in the 1930s, legal rules played an important role in the judicial decision-making process because judges believed that they ought to, for that was the conception of the judicial and legal process that was prevalent. Judges like others are, for want of a better phrase, socialised into accepting the norms of their profession. In the 1930s judges did not have the desire to make policy or to give legal embodiment to their personal policy predilections, and if they had such a desire they believed it should be controlled. This view of the judicial function did not go unchallenged during the 1930s. Legal realism, for reasons that are difficult to locate, did not have a profound impact on the legal profession, particularly amongst academic lawyers.[11] Perhaps realism's appeal was, as Thurman Arnold has written, that 'a realistic jurisprudence is a good medicine for a sick and troubled society. The America of the nineteen thirties was such a society.'[12] But while the appeal of realism cannot be located with any precision, the consequences of its attractions are readily apparent. Realist doctrine, as outlined briefly in Chapter 1, had little regard for the importance of legal rules and it encouraged judges to ignore rules and to make policy. Consequently it is not surprising, given the impact of realism on the legal profession, that some judges by the 1950s, if not earlier, while they were not full-blooded rule-sceptics, did not show the respect for legal rules that was evident among the members of the Supreme Court in the 1930s. Furthermore, these judges made policy, and it is interesting to note that they made little attempt to disguise the fact.[13]

This inevitably raises the question: what is wrong with judicial policy-making? This question in turn raises a broader question: on what basis should the judiciary exercise its considerable power in the American constitutional context? The first question is relatively easy to answer. There are several things wrong with judicial policy-making. The first is that federal judges are the most inappropriate individuals to make public policy. They are isolated from the body politic. They have no contact, no real intimacy with the wider public. Supreme Court justices do not have a structured mechanism for divining public opinion. They do not run for office. Thus they do not and cannot know what people want. The second reason why judicial policy-making is wrong is that if judges want to be legislators they must accept the limitations that restrict the freedom of politicians. Legislators are controlled by the electoral process. They have to appear before and receive the approval of the electorate in order to continue in office. If the federal judiciary do not wish to enter the electoral process they should cease being legislators, for the alternative of being covert legislators without any electoral controls is a profoundly dangerous one for a constitutional democracy, because it forces the electorate to question its faith in its own ability to control public policy through its elected representatives. Consequently judicial policy-making not only removes legitimate policy options from the reach of the political branches of government, but it also damages the faith of the electorate in the efficacy of politics. It denies the electorate's belief that politics can provide solutions for the problems that concern them. Judicial policy-making is, then, profoundly anti-political and anti-democratic and consequently does not offer an appropriate basis for the exercise of the judicial power. If this is the case, where can suitable criteria for the exercise of the judicial power be located? Many attempts have been made to answer this question, most of which have been unsatisfactory. This book will not even make the attempt to answer the question, but merely intends to suggest that the Supreme Court's response to the New Deal between 1934 and 1936 offers an indication of where these standards should be located.

The dominant characteristic of the decisions made by the Court in the period examined by this book was that they emerged out of a distinctive decision-making process. It was not a political decision-making process. It was a legal and judicial process. The judges made their decisions within a reference of legal rules and these legal rules provided both guidance and limitations to the exercise of the judicial power. Admittedly, the perimeters established by these rules were not precise, but there was broad agreement on the Court over their general location and consequently these rules did impose a very real restriction over the exercise of judicial discretion. The discretion was channelled and limited and this is what distinguishes the Court in the 1930s from, say, the Warren Court, and distinguishes a court from a legislature and a judge from a politician. The Supreme Court's response to the New Deal in those two years was not politically popular, but it was a judicial response and in the final analysis that is all that can be asked of judges.

## NOTES

1 For a useful discussion of precedent see R. Wasserstrom, *The Judicial Decision* (1961), pp. 56–84. See also R. Dworkin, 'Is law a system of rules?' in R. Dworkin (ed.), *The Philosophy of Law* (1977), pp. 38–66.
2 D. Lloyd, *Introduction to Jurisprudence* (1979), pp. 820, 821.
3 1 How, 311 (1843).
4 *Block* v. *Hirsh, 256 US 170 (1921); Marcus Brown Holding Co.* v. *Feldman, 256 US 170 (1921); Levi Leasing Co.* v. *Siegel, 258 US 242 (1922).*
5 E. Levi, *An Introduction to Legal Reasoning* (1948), p. 1.
6 94 US 113 (1877).
7 262 US 522 (1923).
8 277 US 350 (1928).
9 The two other dissenters in *Blaisdell* and *Nebbia* were Justices Butler and Van Devanter. It is difficult to assess Van Devanter's ability as he did remarkably little writing but Butler's prose style was never better than turgid and he betrayed a somewhat lumpen quality of mind in his opinions.
10 300 US 379 (1937).
11 W. Rumble, *American Legal Realism* (1968), p. 53.
12 T. Arnold, 'Professor Hart's theology', 73 *Harvard Law Review* 1331, 1334 (1960).
13 This is a reference to the Warren Court. The literature is extensive but see in particular A. Bickel, *The Supreme Court and the Idea of Progress* (1970).

# Bibliography

F. L. Allen, *Since Yesterday* (New York, 1942)

F. L. Allen, 'New Deal honeymoon' in M. Crane (ed.), *The Roosevelt Era* (New York, 1947)

M. Aronson, 'Tendencies in American jurisprudence', 4 *University of Toronto Law Journal* 92 (1941)

J. Auerbach, *Unequal Justice* (New York, 1977)

L. Baker, Back to Back: *The Duel Between FDR and the Supreme Court* (New York, 1967)

T. L. Becker, *Political Behaviouralism and Modern Jurisprudence* (New York, 1964)

M. R. Benedict, *Farm Policies of the United States 1790–1950* (New York, 1953)

R. Berger, *Government by Judiciary: The Transformation of the Fourteenth Amendment* (Cambridge, MA, 1977)

L. E. Beth, *The Development of the American Constitution, 1877–1917* (New York, 1971)

A. Bickel, *The Least Dangerous Branch* (Indianapolis, IN, 1962)

A. Bickel, *The Supreme Court and the Idea of Progress* (New York, 1970)

W. Blackstone, *Commentaries on the Laws of England*, Vol. 3 (London, 1821)

Irving Brant, *Storm over the Constitution (New York, 1936)*

Solon J. Buck, *The Granger Movement* (1933)

J. M. Burns, *Roosevelt: The Lion and the Fox* (London, 1956)

E. Cahn, *Confronting Injustice* (London, 1967)

C. Campbell, *The Farm Bureau and the New Deal* (Urbana, IL, 1962)

B. Cardozo, *The Nature of the Judicial Process* (New Haven, CT, 1921)

M. Cohen, *Reason and Law* (New York, 1961)

R. C. Cortner, *The Jones & Laughlin Case* (1970)

E. S. Corwin, *The Commerce Power Versus States' Rights* (Princeton, NJ, 1936)

E. S. Corwin, *Constitutional Revolution Ltd* (Claremont, NH, 1941)

E. S. Corwin, *Liberty Against Government* (Baton Rouge, LA, 1948)

A. Cox, *The Role of the Supreme Court in American Government* (New York, 1976)

R. Dahl, 'The behaviouralist approach to political science: an epitaph for a monument to a successful protest', 55 *American Political Science Review* 763 (1961)

D. Danelski, 'The influence of the Chief Justice in the decisional process' in W. Murphy and C. Pritchett (eds.), *Courts, Judges and Politics* (1961)

# Bibliography

R. Dworkin (ed.), *The Philosophy of Law* (1977)

E. Erikson, *Supreme Court and the New Deal* (Los Angeles, CA, 1941)

C. Fairman, 'The so-called Granger Cases', V *Stanford Law Review* 592 (1953)

C. Fairman, *History of the Supreme Court of the United States: Reconstruction and Reunion. 1964–88 Part One* (New York, 1971)

S. Fine, *Laissez-Faire and the General Welfare State* (Ann Arbor, MI, 1956)

G. Fite, *George N. Peek and the Fight for Farm Parity* (Norman, OK, 1954)

J. Frank, 'A lawyer looks at language' in S. L. Hayakawa (ed.), *Language in Action* (1941)

J. Frank, *Courts on Trial: Myth and Reality in American Justice* (Princeton, NJ, 1949)

J. Frank, *Law and the Modern Mind* (New York, 1930 and 1963)

F. Frankfurther, *The Commerce Clause Under Marshall, Taney and Waite* (Chapel Hill, NC, 1937)

F. Frankfurther, 'Mr Justice Roberts', 104 *University of Pennsylvania Law Review*, 313 (1955)

M. Freedman (ed.), *Roosevelt and Frankfurther: Their Correspondence 1928–1945* (Boston, MA, 1967)

M. Freedman and A. J. Schwarz, *A Monetary History of the United States 1876–1970* (1971)

P. Freund, *The Supreme Court of the US: Business, Purpose, Performance* (Cleveland, OH, 1961)

P. Freund, *On Law and Justice* (Cambridge, MA, 1968)

P. Freund, 'Charles Evans Hughes as Chief Justice', 81 *Harvard Law Review* 16 (1968)

L. Fuller, 'An afterword: science and the judicial process', 79 *Harvard Law Review* 1604 (1966)

B. Gavit, *The Commerce Clause of the United States Constitution* (1932)

E. Gerhart, *America's Advocate: Robert H. Jackson* (Indianapolis, IN, 1958)

H. J. Graham, *Everyman's Constitution: Historical Essays on The Fourteenth Amendment, the 'Conspiracy Theory' and American Constitutionalism* (1968)

J. B. Grossman, 'Role-playing and the analysis of judicial behaviour: the case of Mr Justice Frankfurther', 11 *Journal of Public Law* 285 (1962)

J. B. Grossman and J. Tannenhaus (eds.), *Frontiers of Judicial Research* (1969)

Arnold Bennet Hall, 'Round table on public law', 20 *American Political Science Review* 1927 (1926)

M. Hall (ed.), *Selected Writings of Benjamin Nathan Cardozo* (1947)

H. Hart, 'Holmes's positivism – an addendum', 64 *Harvard Law Review* 530 (1951)

E. Hawley, *The New Deal and the Problem of Monopoly* (Princeton, NJ, 1966)

S. Hendel, *Charles Evans Hughes and the Supreme Court* (New York, 1951)

R. D. Henson (ed.), *Landmarks of Law* (Boston, MA, 1960)

O. W. Holmes, *The Common Law* (Boston, MA, 1881)

O. W. Holmes, 'The path of the law', 10 *Harvard Law Review* 458 (1897)

M. D. Howe, 'The positivism of Mr Justice Holmes', 64 *Harvard Law Review* 530 (1951)

M. D. Howe, 'Holmes's positivism – a brief rejoinder', 64 *Harvard Law Review* 530 (1951)

R. F. Howell, 'The judicial conservatives three decades ago: aristocratic guardians of the prerogatives of property and the judiciary', 4 *Virginia Law Review* 1447 (1963)

D. Ingersoll, 'Karl Llewellyn, American legal realism and contemporary legal behaviouralism, 76 *Ethics* 253 (1966)

R. H. Jackson, *The Struggle for Judicial Supremacy* (New York, 1955)

J. B. James, *The Framing of the Fourteenth Amendment* (Urbana, IL, 1956)

H. Johnson, *The Blue Eagle From Egg to Earth* (New York, 1935)

S. J. Konefsky, *Chief Justice Stone and the Supreme Court* (New York, 1945)

P. Kurland, *Politics, The Constitution and the Warren Court* (1970)

J. Lash, *From the Diaries of Felix Frankfurter* (New York, 1975)

P. Laslett (ed.), *John Locke: Two Treatises of Government* (1963)

C. A. Leonard, *A Search for a Judicial Philosophy: Mr Justice Roberts and the Constitutional Revolution of 1937* (Port Washington, NY, 1971)

W. Letwin, *A Documentary History of American Economic Policy* (1961)

W. E. Leuchtenburg, 'The origins of Franklin D. Roosevelt's 'court-packing' plan', *The Supreme Court Review 1966* (Chicago, IL, 1967)

E. Levi, *An Introduction to Legal Reasoning* (1948)

L. Levy (ed.), *American Constitutional Law* (New York, 1966)

K. Llewellyn, *The Common Law Tradition* (Boston, MA, 1960)

K. Llewellyn, *Jurisprudence: Realism in Theory and Practice* (Chicago, IL, 1962)

D. Lloyd, *Introduction to Jurisprudence* (1979)

C. P. Magrath, *Morrison R. Waite: The Triumph of Character* (1963)

J. McClellan, *Joseph Story and the American Constitution* (1971)

R. G. McCloskey, *American Conservatism in the Age of Enterprise* (New York, 1951)

R. G. McCloskey (ed.), *Essays in Constitutional Law* (New York, 1957)

R. G. McCloskey, 'Economic due process and the Supreme Court: An exhumation and reburial' in L. Levy (ed.), *American Constitutional Law* (New York, 1966)

R. G. McCloskey, *The Modern Supreme Court* (Chicago, IL, 1972)

R. A. Maidment, 'Law and economic policy in the United States', 7 *Journal of Legal History* 196 (1986)

R. A. Maidment, 'The New Deal Court revisited' in S. Baskerville and R.

# Bibliography

Willett (eds.), *Nothing Else to Fear* (Manchester, 1987)

G. Marshall, *Constitutional Theory* (Oxford, 1971)

A. T. Mason, 'The conservative world of Mr Justice Sutherland, 1883–1910', 32 *American Political Science Review* 443 (1938)

A. T. Mason, *Brandeis: A Free Man's Life* (New York, 1946)

A. T. Mason, *Harlan F. Stone: Pillar of the Law* (New York, 1956)

A. T. Mason, *The Supreme Court from Taft to Warren* (Baton Rouge, LA, 1964)

W. Mendelson, 'The untroubled world of jurimetrics', 26 *Journal of Politics* 914 (1964)

W. Mendelson, *Justices Black and Frankfurter: Conflict in the Court* (Chicago, IL, 1966)

W. Mendelson, *The Supreme Court: Law and Discretion* (1967)

A. S. Miller, *The Supreme Court and American Capitalism* (New York, 1968)

A. S. Miller and R. F. Howell, 'The myth of neutrality in constitutional adjudication', 27 *University of Chicago Law Review* 661 (1960)

C. A. Miller, *The Supreme Court and the Uses of History* (Cambridge, MA, 1969)

S. F. Miller, *Lectures on the Constitution* (New York, 1893)

R. Moley, *After Seven Years* (New York, 1939)

Baron de Montesquieu, *The Spirit of the* Lois (London, 1900)

W. Murphy, *Congress and the Court* (Chicago, IL, 1962)

W. Murphy, *Elements of Judicial Strategy* (1964)

S. Nagel, 'Political party affiliation and judges' decisions' 55 *American Political Science Review* (1961)

S. Nagel, 'Ethnic affiliation and judicial propensities', 24 *Journal of Politics*, 92 (1962)

S. Nagel, 'Testing relations between judicial characteristics and judicial decision-making', 15 *Western Political Quarterly* 425 (1962)

J. F. Paschal, *Mr Justice Sutherland: A Man Against the State* (Princeton, NJ, 1951)

A. M. Paul, *Conservative Crisis and the Rule of Law* (New York, 1969)

D. Pearson and R. Allen, *The Nine Old Men* (New York, 1937)

D. Perkins, *The New Age of Franklin Roosevelt* (Chicago, IL, 1956)

V. Perkins, *Crisis in Agriculture* (Berkeley, CA, 1969)

C. H. Pritchett, *The Roosevelt Court: A Study in Judicial Politics and Values 1937–1947* (Chicago, IL, 1969)

C. H. Pritchett, 'The development of judicial research', in J. B. Grossman and H. Tannenhaus (eds.), *Frontiers of Judicial Research* (1969)

M. Pusey, *Charles Evans Hughes* (New York, 1952)

B. Rauch, *The History of the New Deal* (New York, 1963)

B. Rauch (ed.), *Franklin D. Roosevelt: Selected Speeches, Messages, Press Conferences and Letters* (New York, 1964)

M. Richter, *The Political Theory of Montesquieu* (Cambridge, 1977)

F. Rodell, *Nine Men: A Political History of the Supreme Court of the United States from 1790 to 1955* (New York, 1955)

F. Rodell, 'For every justice judicial defence is a sometime thing', 50 *Georgetown Law Journal*, (1962)

P. Rosen, *The Supreme Court and Social Science* (Urbana, IL, 1972)

W. Rowley, *M. L. Wilson and the Campaign for Domestic Allotment* (Lincoln, NB, 1970)

W. Rumble, Jr, *American Legal Realism* (Ithaca, NY, 1968)

A. Schlesinger Jr, *The Coming of the New Deal* (Boston, MA, 1965)

A. Schlesinger Jr, *The Politics of Upheaval* (Boston, MA, 1966)

J. Schmidhauser, 'The justices of the Supreme Court: a collective portrait', 3 *Midwest Journal of Political Science* 1 (1959)

J. Schmidhauser, *The Supreme Court: Its Politics, Personalities and Procedures* (New York, 1960)

G. Schubert, *Judicial Policy-Making* (Glenview, IL, 1966)

G. Schubert, 'The nineteen sixty term of the Supreme Court: a psychological analysis', 56 *American Political Science Review* 90 (1962)

G. Schubert, *Constitutional Politics* (New York, 1964)

B. Schwartz, *American Constitutional Law* (New York, 1955)

B. Schwartz, *A Commentary on the Constitution of the United States, The Powers of Government* Vol. I (1963)

B. Schwartz, *A Commentary on the Constitution of the United States, The Powers of Government* Vol. II (1964)

J. Shideler, *Farm Crisis, 1919–1923* (1957)

J. D. Sprague, *Voting Patterns on the United States Supreme Court: Cases in Federalism 1889–1959* (1968)

J. Story, *Commentaries on the Constitutions of the United States* (1883)

A. E. Sutherland, *Constitutionalism in America* (New York, 1965)

C. B. Swisher, *Growth of Constitutional Power in the United States* (Chicago, IL, 1946)

J. Tannenhaus, 'Supreme Court attitudes toward federal administrative agencies, 1947–1956: an application of social science methods to the study of the judicial process', 14 *Vanderbilt Law Review* 473 (1961)

J. Tannenhaus, 'Cumulative scaling of judicial decisions', 79 *Harvard Law Review* 1583 (1966)

R. Tugwell, *The Democratic Roosevelt* (New York, 1957)

R. Tugwell, *The Battle of Democracy* (1935)

R. Tugwell, *The Democratic Roosevelt* (New York, 1957)

W. Twining, *Karl Llewellyn and the Realist Movement* (1973)

B. Twiss, *Lawyers and the Constitution* (Princeton, NJ, 1942)

M. J. C. Vile, *Constitutionalism and the Separation of Powers* (Oxford, 1967)

R. Wasserstrom, *The Judicial Decision: Towards a Theory of Legal*

# Bibliography

Justification (Stanford, IN, 1961)

H. Wechsler, 'Toward neutral principles of constitutional law', 73 *Harvard Law Review* 1 (1959)

H. Wechsler, *Principles, Politics and Fundamental Law* (1961)

G. White, *The American Judicial Tradition* (New York, 1976)

S. Wolin, 'Paradigms and political theories' in P. King and B. C. Parekh (eds.), *Politics and Experience: Essays Presented to Professor Michael Oakeshott on the Occasion of his Retirement* (1968)

B. F. Wright, *Growth of American Constitutional Law* (New York, 1942)

B. M. Ziegler, *The Supreme Court and American Economic Life* (Evanston, IL, 1962)

# Cases cited

Adair v. United States, 208 US 161 (1908)
Amazon Petroleum Corp. et al. v. Ryan et al., 293 US 388 (1935)
Ashton v. Cameron County Dist., 298 US 513 (1936)
Ashwander v. Tennessee Valley Authority, 297 US 288 (1936)
Bailey v. Drexel-Furniture Co., 259 US 20 (1922)
Baker v. Carr, 369 US 186 (1962)
Barnitz v. Beverly, 163 US 118 (1896)
Block v. Hirsh, 256 US 170 (1921)
Bronson v. Kinzie, 1 How. 311 (1843)
Bronson v. Rodes, 7 Wall. 229 (1869)
Brown v. Board of Education of Topeka, 347 US 483 (1954)
Bunting v. Oregon, 243 US 246 (1917)
Carter v. Carter Coal Co., 298 US 238 (1936)
Chas. Wolff Packing Co. v. Industrial Court, 262 US 522 (1923)
Dayton-Goose Creek Railway Co. v. United States, 263 US 456 (1924)
Fletcher v. Peck, 6 Cranch 87 (1810)
Gibbons v. Ogden, 9 Wheat. 1 (1824)
Gregory v. Morris, 98 US 619 (1878)
Hammer v. Dagenhart, 247 US 251 (1918)
Hepburn v. Griswold, 8 Wall. 603 (1870)
Hill v. Wallace, 259 US 44 (1922)
Holden v. Hardy, 169 US 366 (1898)
Home Building and Loan Association v. Blaisdell, 290 US 398 (1934)
Hopkins Federal Savings and Loan Association v. Cleary et al., 296 US
      315 (1935)
Houston, E.&W. Texas Railway v. United States, 234 US 342 (1914)
Howard v. Bugbee, 23 How. 461 (1860)
Hudson Water Co. v. McCarter, 209 US 349 (1908)
Jones v. Securities Exchange Commission, 298 US 1 (1936)
Juillard v. Greenman, 110 US 421 (1884)
Kidd v. Pearson, 128 US 1 (1888)
Legal Tender Cases, 12 Wall. 457 (1871)
Levi Leasing Co. v. Siegel, 258 US 242 (1922)
License Cases, 5 How. 504 (1847)
Ling Su Fan v. United States *218 US 302 (1910)*
*Lochner v.* New York, 198 US 45 (1905)
Louisville Joint Stock Land Bank v. Radford, 295 US 555 (1935)
Marcus Brown Holding Co. v. Feldman, 256 US 179 (1921)
Massachusetts v. Mellon, 262 US 447 (1923)
McCulloch v. Maryland, 4 Wheat. 316 (1819)

# Cases cited

Minersville School District v. Gobitis, 310 US 586 (1940)
Minnesota v. Blasius, 290 US 1 (1933)
Minnesota Rate Case, 134 US 418 (1890)
Miranda v. Arizona, 384 US 436 (1966)
Missouri v. Holland, 252 US 416 (1920)
Morehead v. New York ex rel. Tipaldo, 298 US 587 (1936)
Mountain Timber Co. v. Washington, 243 US 219 (1917)
Muller v. Oregon, 208 US 412 (1908)
Munn v. Illinois, 94 US 113 (1877)
National Labor Relations Board v. Jones & Laughlin Steel Corp., 301 US 1 (1937)
Nebbia v. New York, 291 US 502 (1934)
Norman v. Baltimore and Ohio Railroad Co., 294 US 240 (1935)
Nortz v. United States, 294 US 317 (1935)
Oliver Iron Co. v. Lord, 262 US 172 (1923)
Panama Refining Co. et al. v. Ryan et al., 293 US 388 (1935)
Peck v. C & N.W.R. Co., 94 US 164 (1877)
People v. Nebbia, 262 N.Y. 259 (1933)
Perry v. United States, 294 US 330 (1935)
Plessy v. Ferguson, 163 US 537 (1896)
Pollock v. Farmers' Loan and Trust Co., 157 US 429 (1895)
Railroad Co. v. Richmond, 96 US 521 (1878)
Railroad Retirement Board et al. v. Alton Railroad Co. et al., 295 US 330 (1935)
Ribnik v. McBride, 277 US 350 (1928)
A. L. A. Schechter Poultry Corporation v. United States, 295 US 495 (1935)
Sinking-Fund Cases, 99 US 700 (1879)
Slaughter-house Cases, 16 Wall. 36 (1873)
Smyth v. Ames, 169 US 466 (1898)
Stafford v. Wallace, 258 US 495 (1922)
Stetler v. O'Hara, 243 US 649 (1917)
Stone v. Farmers' Loan and Trust Co., 116 US 307 (1886)
Swift and Co. v. United States, 196 U.S. 375 (1905)
Trebilcock v. Wilson, 12 Wall. 687 (1871)
Triegle v. Acme Homestead Association, 279 U.S. 189 (1936)
Tyson & Bro. – United Theatre Ticket Officers v. Banton, 273 U.S. 418 (1927)
United States v. Belcher, 294 U.S. 736 (1935)
United States v. Butler, 297 U.S. 1 (1936)
United States v. Constantine, 296 U.S. 287 (1935)
United States v. Grimaud, 220 U.S. 506 (1911)
United States v. Insurance Companies, 22 Wall. 99 (1874)

United States *v.* E. C. Knight Co., 156 U.S. 1 (1895)
West Coast Hotel *v.* Parrish, 300 U.S. 379 (1937)
West Virginia State Board of Education *v.* Barnette, 319 U.S. 624 (1943)
Worthen Co. *v.* Kavanaugh, 295 U.S. 56 (1935)
Worthen Co. *v.* Thomas, 292 U.S. 426 (1934)

# Index

# Index